rude mechs'
LIPSTICK
TRACES

53SP 31
March 2019
Brooklyn, NY

53rdstatepress.org

Rude Mechs' Lipstick Traces

A graphic adaptation by Lana Lesley of the stage adaptation by Rude Mechs of the book **Lipstick Traces: A Secret History of the Twentieth Century** Copyright © 1989 by Greil Marcus. Printed with permission of Greil Marcus and Harvard University Press.

This publication of **Rude Mechs' Lipstick Traces**, by Lana Lesley, through 53rd State Press, is made possible by 53rd State Press in partnership with Rude Mechanicals A Theatre Collective (aka Rude Mechs) and by the New York State Council on the Arts with the support of Governor Andrew M. Cuomo and the New York State Legislature.

Book design, composition, and illustrations by Lana Lesley

ISBN no. 978-0-9817533-2-4

Printed in the United States of America on recycled paper. Illustrations were inked with Prismacolor pens, Sakura Gelly Roll pens, and Sharpie markers and drawn on copy paper.

53rd State books are available to the trade through TCG (Theatre Communications Group) and are distributed by Consortium: https://www.cbsd.com.

a graphic adaptation
by
Lana Lesley
of
the stage adaptation
by
Rude Mechs
of
Lipstick Traces: A Secret History of the Twentieth Century
by
Greil Marcus

for Peter

rude mechs'
LIPSTICK
TRACES

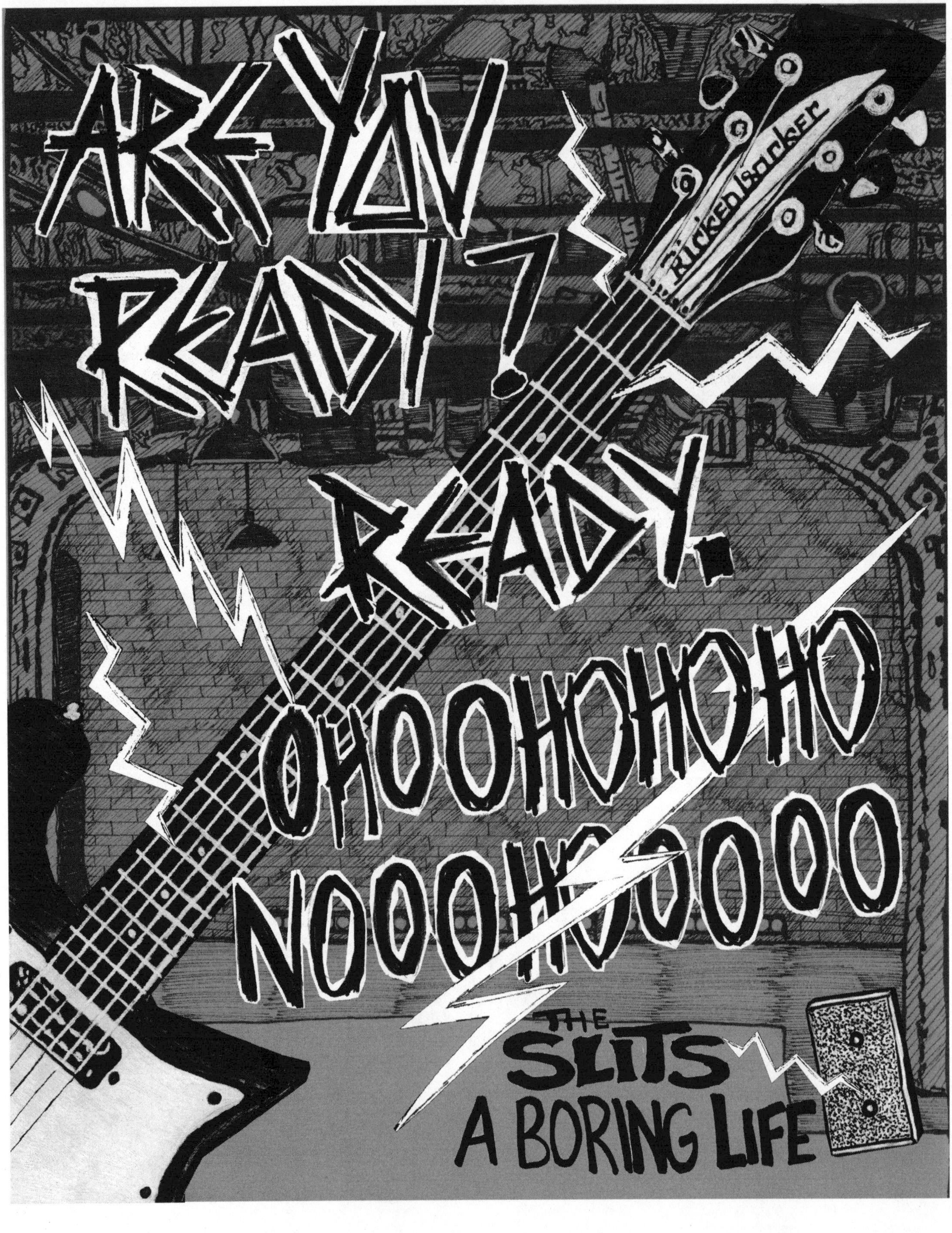
ARE YOU READY?
READY.
OHOOHOHOHOHO
NOOOHOOOOOO
THE SLITS
A BORING LIFE
Rickenbacker

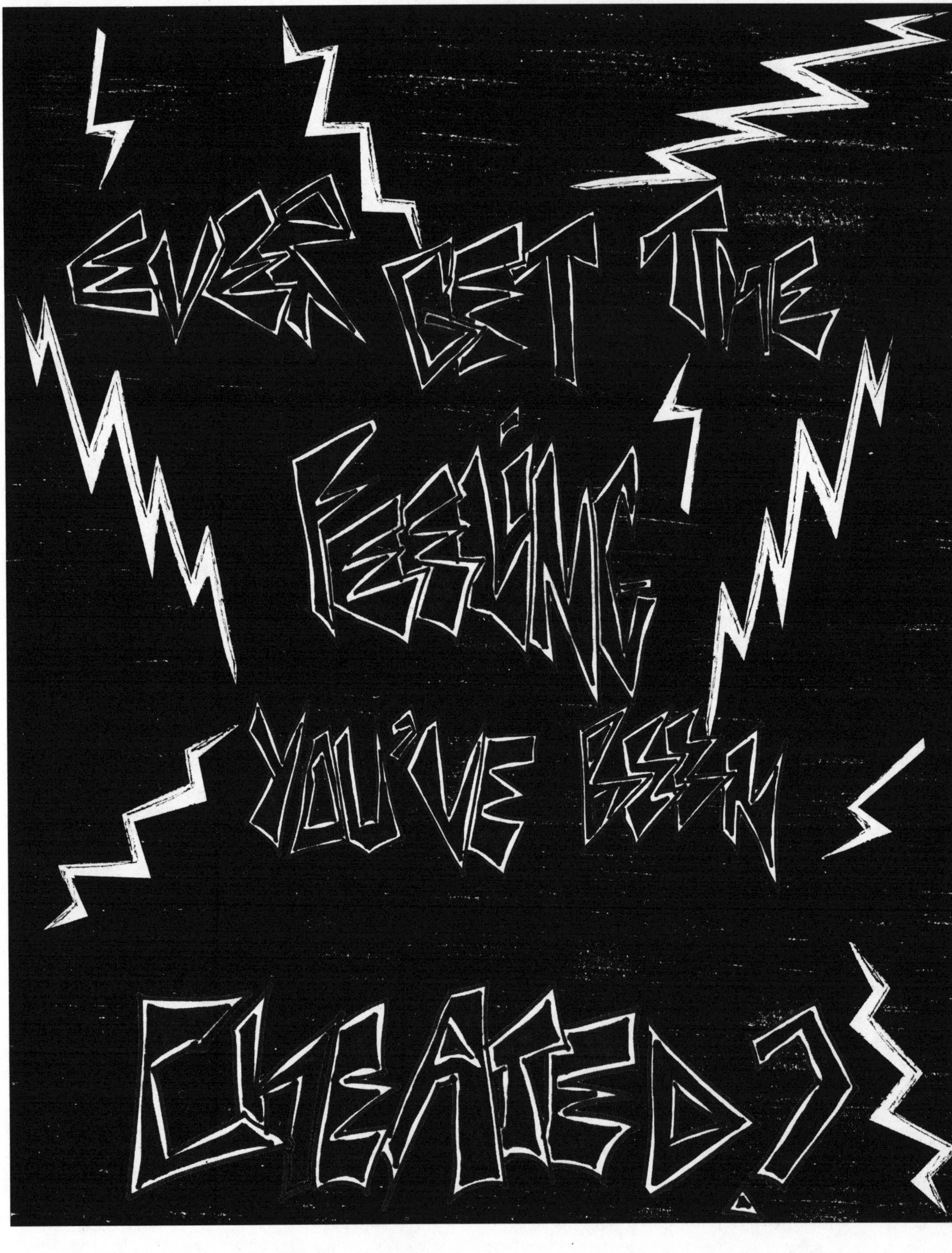
EVER GET THE
FEELING
YOU'VE BEEN
CHEATED?

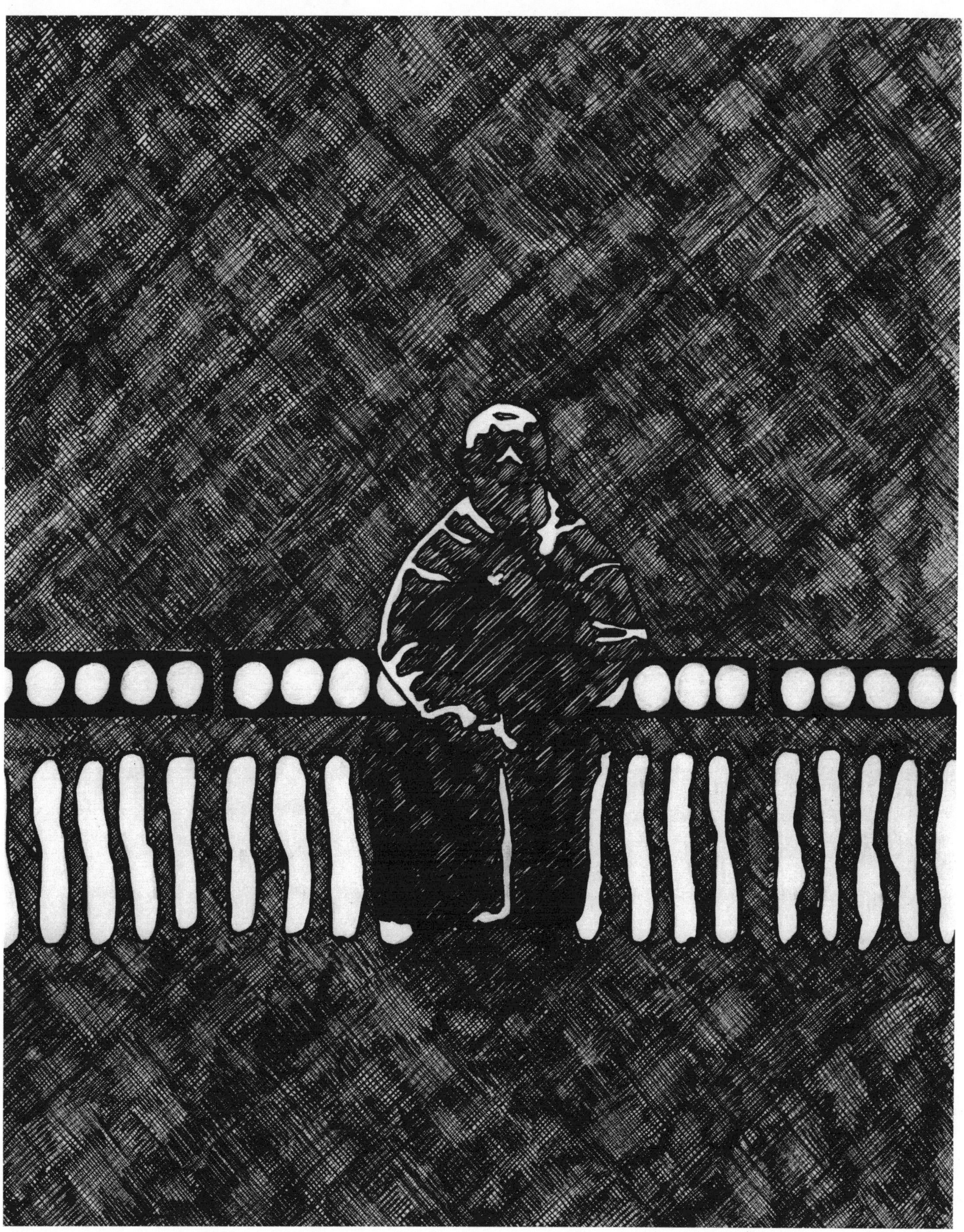

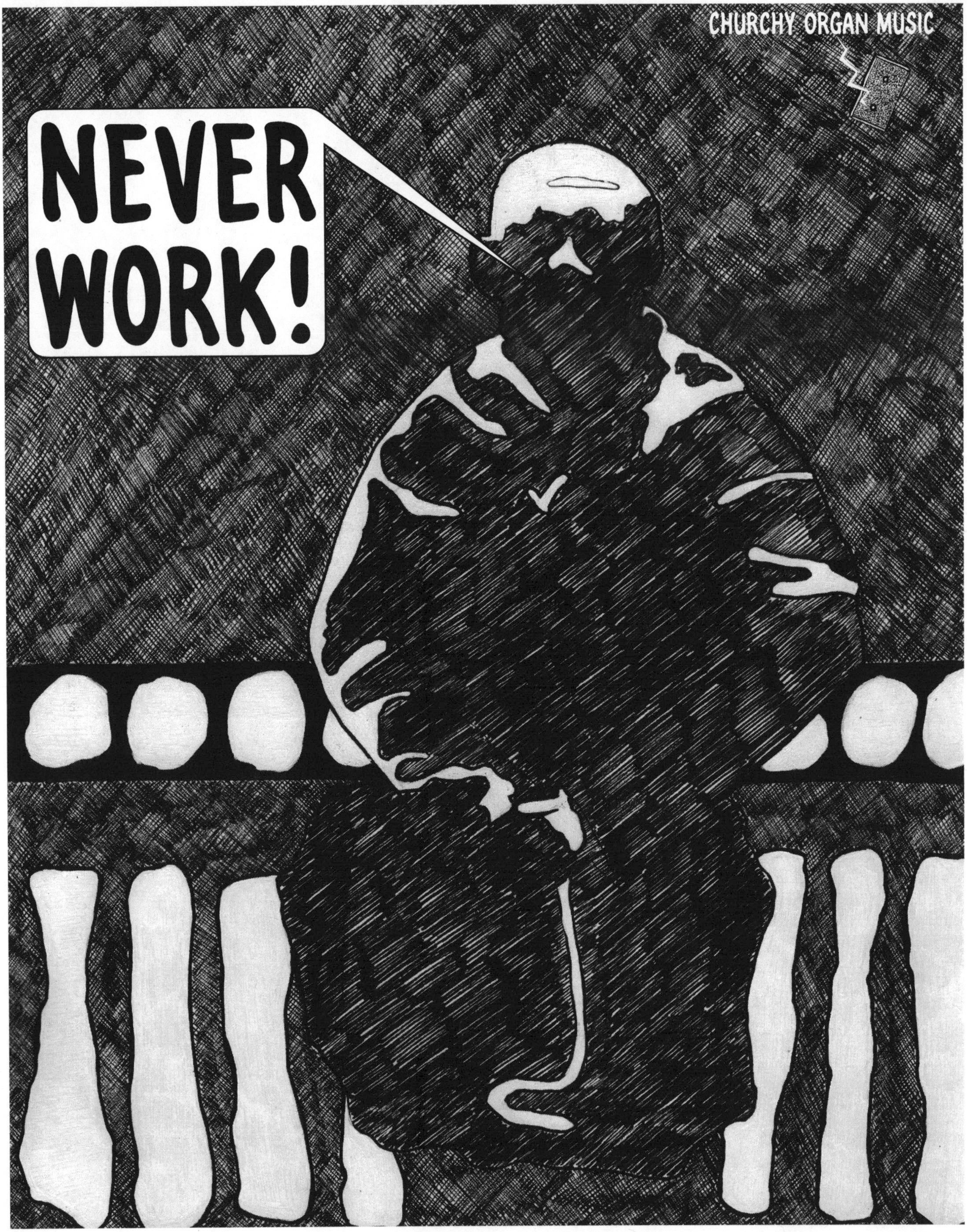
CHURCHY ORGAN MUSIC
NEVER WORK!

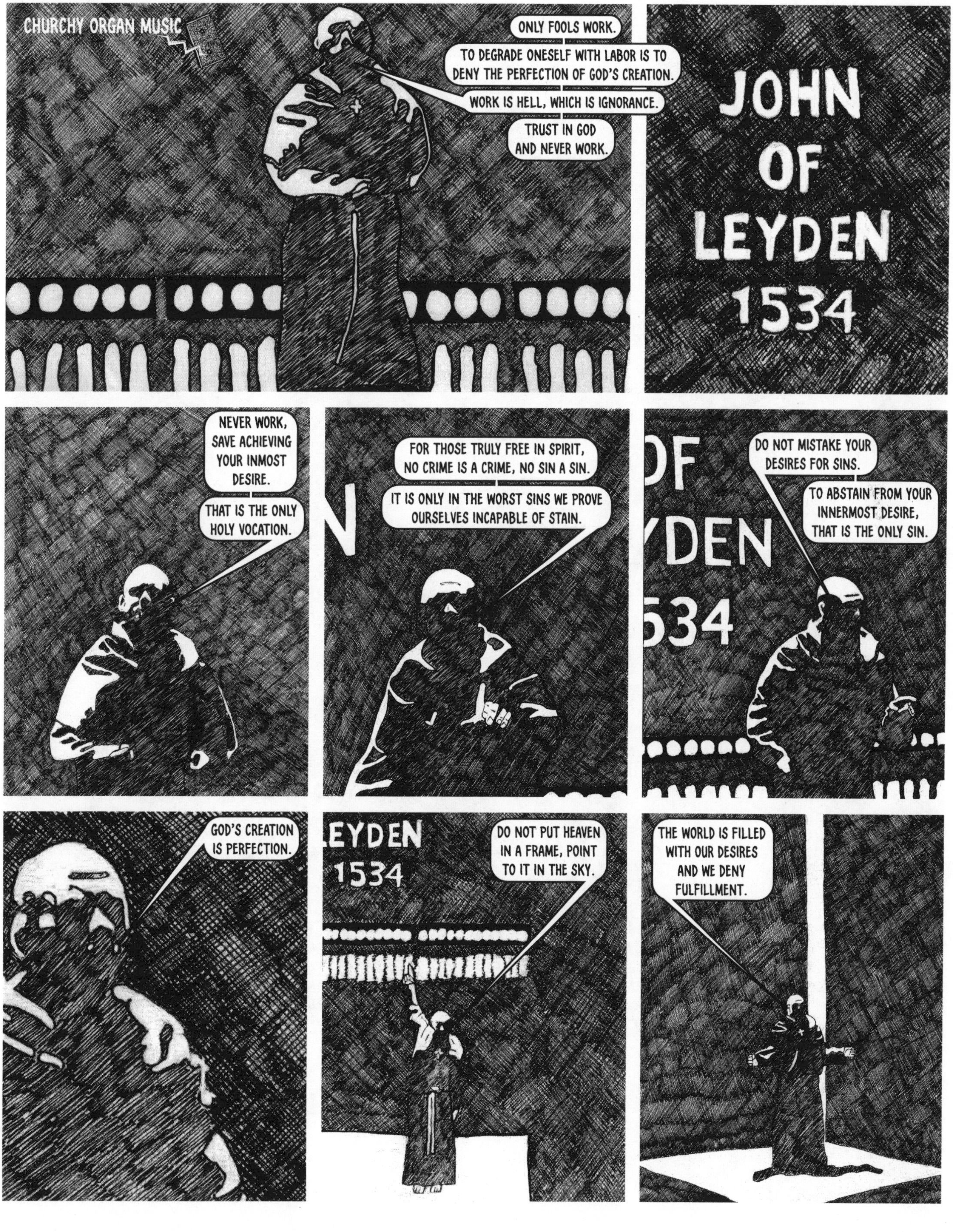
CHURCHY ORGAN MUSIC
ONLY FOOLS WORK.
TO DEGRADE ONESELF WITH LABOR IS TO DENY THE PERFECTION OF GOD'S CREATION.
WORK IS HELL, WHICH IS IGNORANCE.
TRUST IN GOD AND NEVER WORK.
JOHN OF LEYDEN 1534
NEVER WORK, SAVE ACHIEVING YOUR INMOST DESIRE.
THAT IS THE ONLY HOLY VOCATION.
FOR THOSE TRULY FREE IN SPIRIT, NO CRIME IS A CRIME, NO SIN A SIN.
IT IS ONLY IN THE WORST SINS WE PROVE OURSELVES INCAPABLE OF STAIN.
DO NOT MISTAKE YOUR DESIRES FOR SINS.
TO ABSTAIN FROM YOUR INNERMOST DESIRE, THAT IS THE ONLY SIN.
GOD'S CREATION IS PERFECTION.
DO NOT PUT HEAVEN IN A FRAME, POINT TO IT IN THE SKY.
THE WORLD IS FILLED WITH OUR DESIRES AND WE DENY FULFILLMENT.

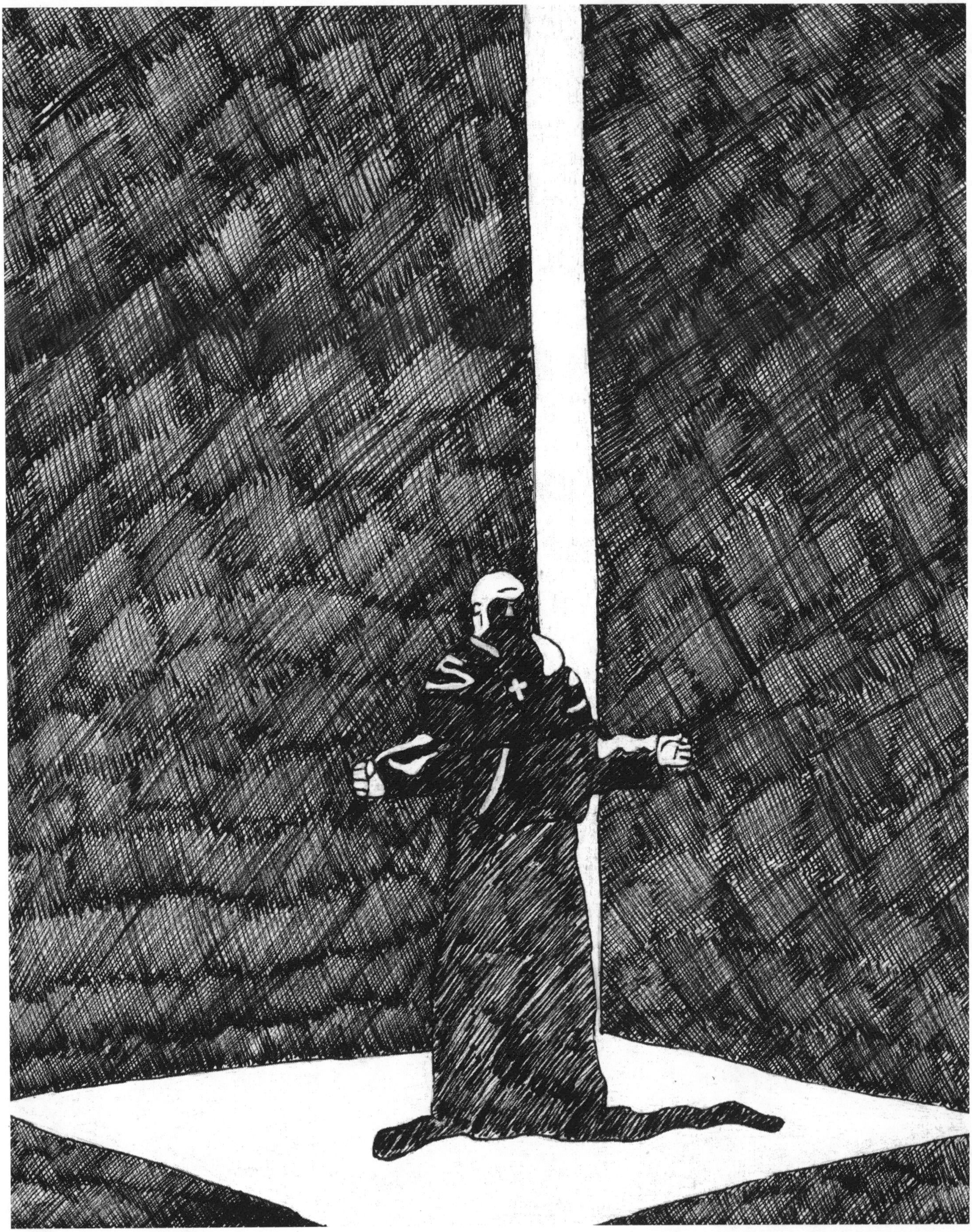

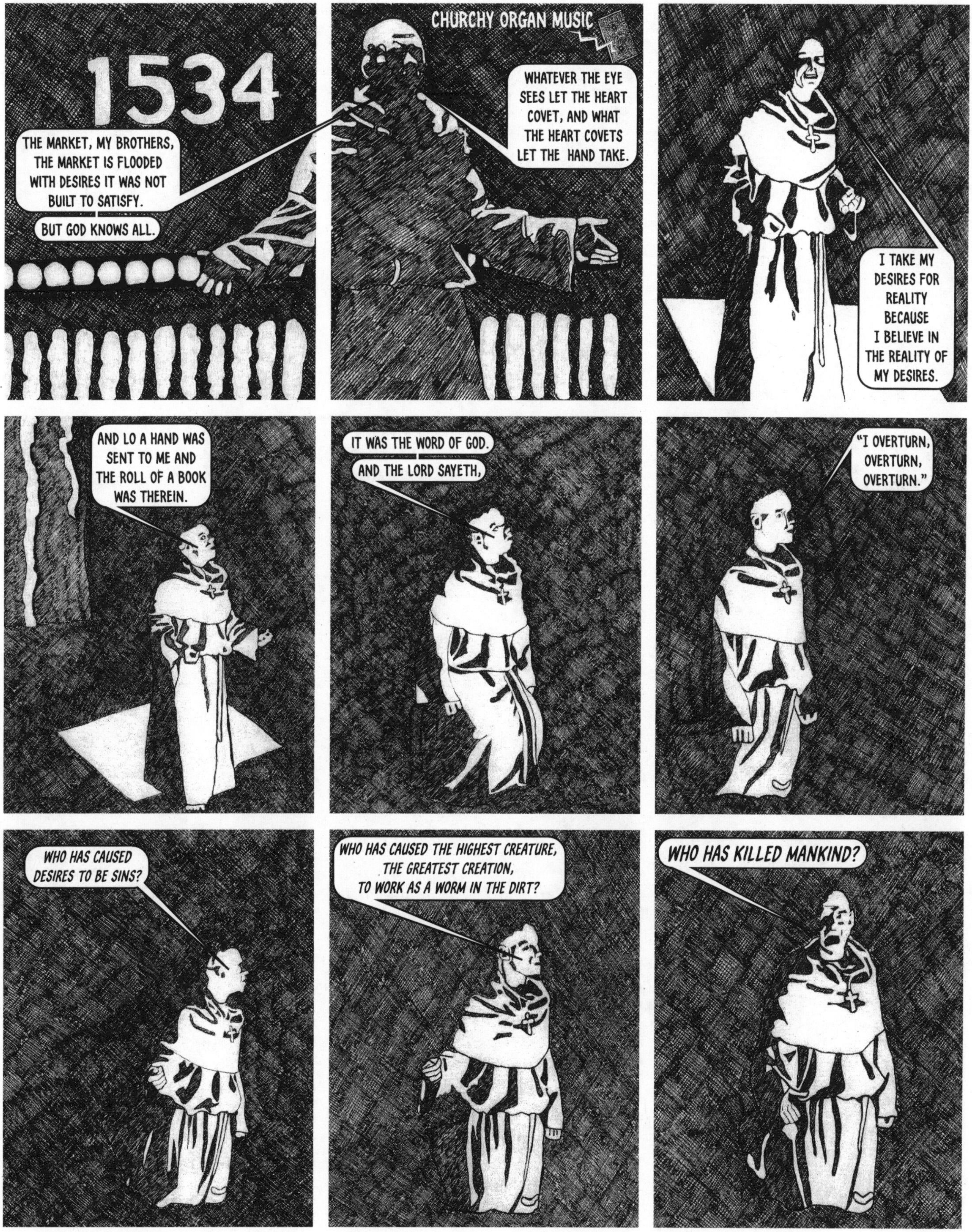
1534
THE MARKET, MY BROTHERS, THE MARKET IS FLOODED WITH DESIRES IT WAS NOT BUILT TO SATISFY.
BUT GOD KNOWS ALL.
CHURCHY ORGAN MUSIC
WHATEVER THE EYE SEES LET THE HEART COVET, AND WHAT THE HEART COVETS LET THE HAND TAKE.
I TAKE MY DESIRES FOR REALITY BECAUSE I BELIEVE IN THE REALITY OF MY DESIRES.
AND LO A HAND WAS SENT TO ME AND THE ROLL OF A BOOK WAS THEREIN.
IT WAS THE WORD OF GOD.
AND THE LORD SAYETH,
"I OVERTURN, OVERTURN, OVERTURN."
WHO HAS CAUSED DESIRES TO BE SINS?
WHO HAS CAUSED THE HIGHEST CREATURE, THE GREATEST CREATION, TO WORK AS A WORM IN THE DIRT?
WHO HAS KILLED MANKIND?

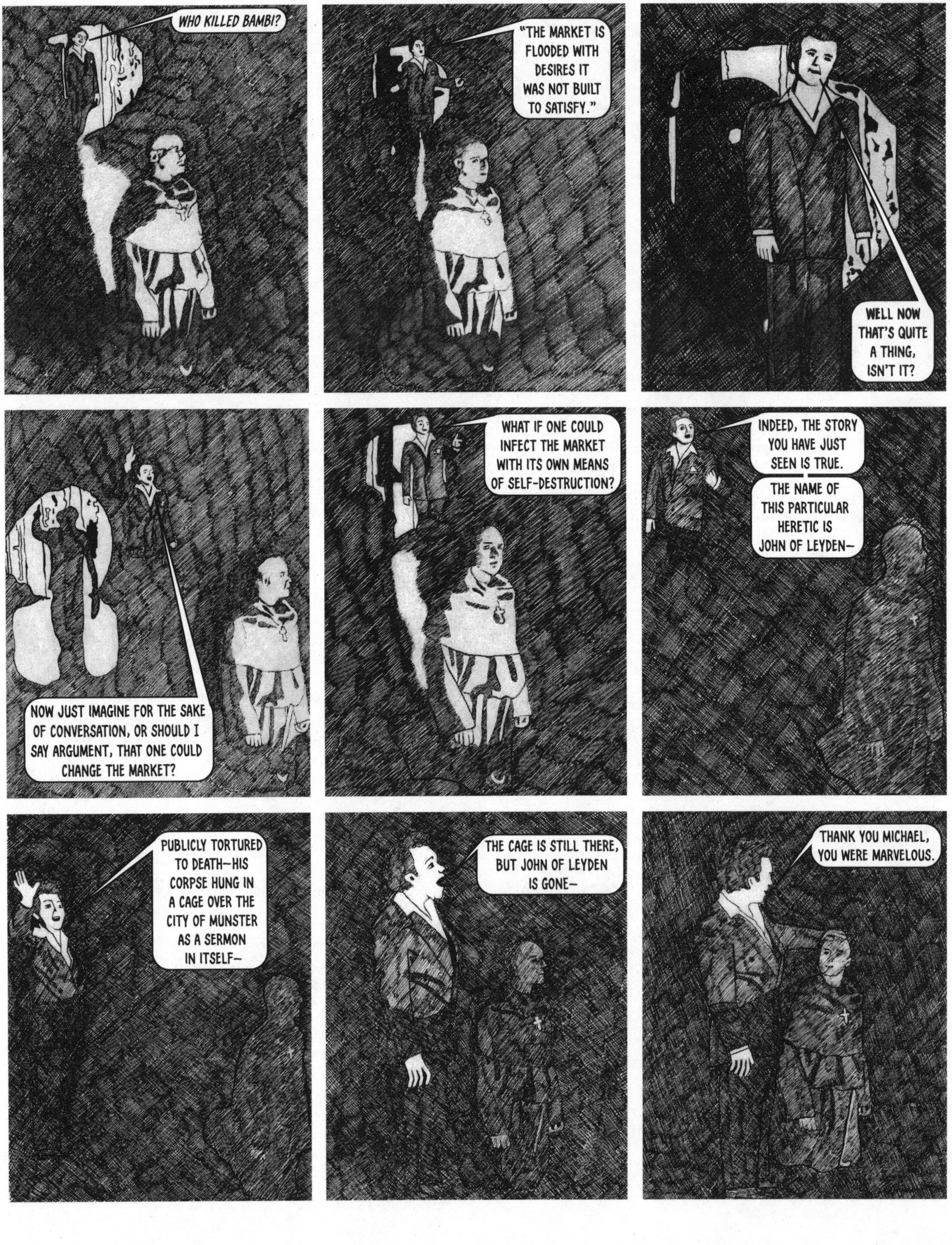
WHO KILLED BAMBI?
"THE MARKET IS FLOODED WITH DESIRES IT WAS NOT BUILT TO SATISFY."
WELL NOW THAT'S QUITE A THING, ISN'T IT?
NOW JUST IMAGINE FOR THE SAKE OF CONVERSATION, OR SHOULD I SAY ARGUMENT, THAT ONE COULD CHANGE THE MARKET?
WHAT IF ONE COULD INFECT THE MARKET WITH ITS OWN MEANS OF SELF-DESTRUCTION?
INDEED, THE STORY YOU HAVE JUST SEEN IS TRUE.
THE NAME OF THIS PARTICULAR HERETIC IS JOHN OF LEYDEN—
PUBLICLY TORTURED TO DEATH—HIS CORPSE HUNG IN A CAGE OVER THE CITY OF MUNSTER AS A SERMON IN ITSELF—
THE CAGE IS STILL THERE, BUT JOHN OF LEYDEN IS GONE—
THANK YOU MICHAEL, YOU WERE MARVELOUS.

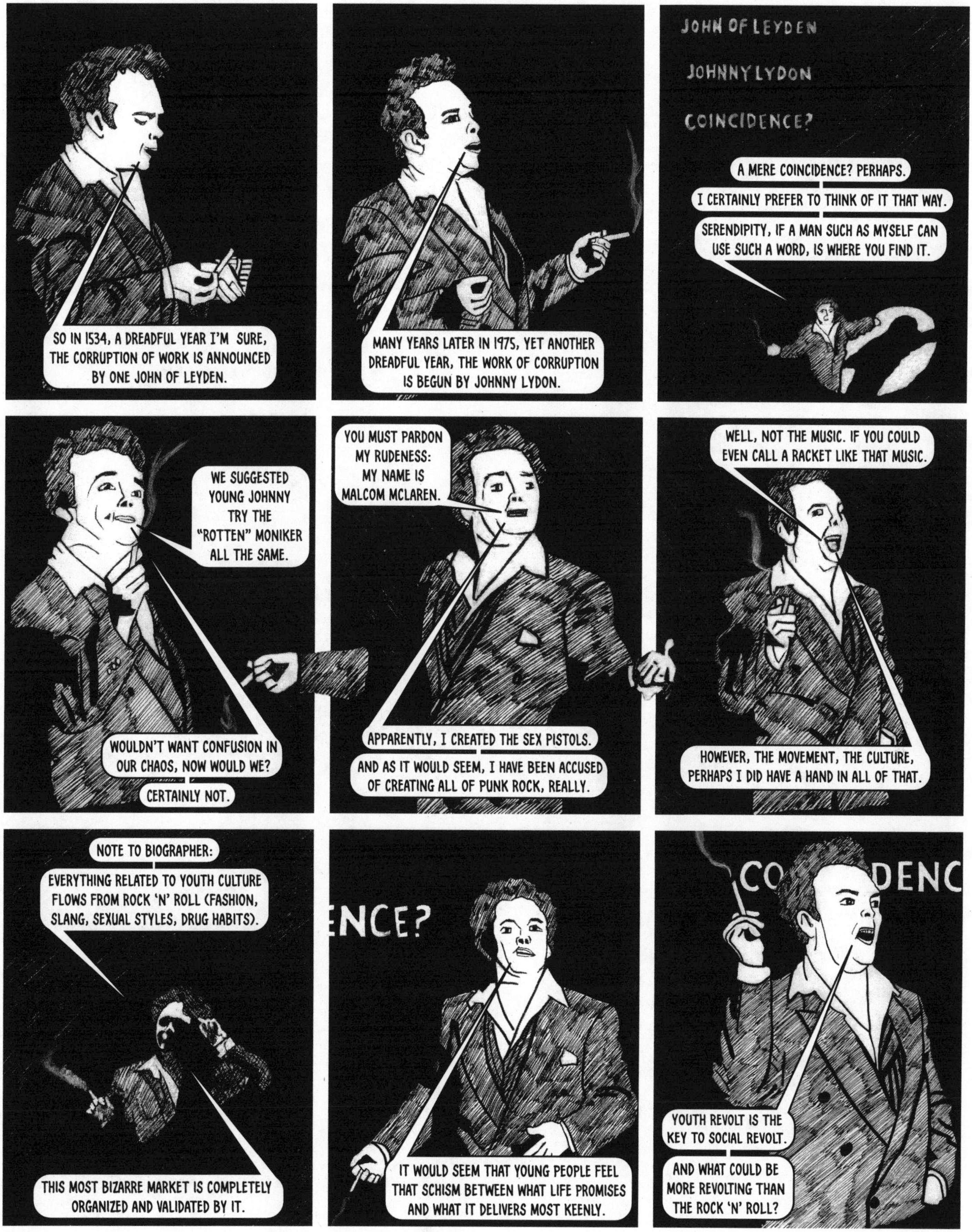
SO IN 1534, A DREADFUL YEAR I'M SURE, THE CORRUPTION OF WORK IS ANNOUNCED BY ONE JOHN OF LEYDEN.
MANY YEARS LATER IN 1975, YET ANOTHER DREADFUL YEAR, THE WORK OF CORRUPTION IS BEGUN BY JOHNNY LYDON.
JOHN OF LEYDEN
JOHNNY LYDON
COINCIDENCE?
A MERE COINCIDENCE? PERHAPS.
I CERTAINLY PREFER TO THINK OF IT THAT WAY.
SERENDIPITY, IF A MAN SUCH AS MYSELF CAN USE SUCH A WORD, IS WHERE YOU FIND IT.
WE SUGGESTED YOUNG JOHNNY TRY THE "ROTTEN" MONIKER ALL THE SAME.
WOULDN'T WANT CONFUSION IN OUR CHAOS, NOW WOULD WE?
CERTAINLY NOT.
YOU MUST PARDON MY RUDENESS: MY NAME IS MALCOM MCLAREN.
APPARENTLY, I CREATED THE SEX PISTOLS.
AND AS IT WOULD SEEM, I HAVE BEEN ACCUSED OF CREATING ALL OF PUNK ROCK, REALLY.
WELL, NOT THE MUSIC. IF YOU COULD EVEN CALL A RACKET LIKE THAT MUSIC.
HOWEVER, THE MOVEMENT, THE CULTURE, PERHAPS I DID HAVE A HAND IN ALL OF THAT.
NOTE TO BIOGRAPHER:
EVERYTHING RELATED TO YOUTH CULTURE FLOWS FROM ROCK 'N' ROLL (FASHION, SLANG, SEXUAL STYLES, DRUG HABITS).
THIS MOST BIZARRE MARKET IS COMPLETELY ORGANIZED AND VALIDATED BY IT.
ENCE?
IT WOULD SEEM THAT YOUNG PEOPLE FEEL THAT SCHISM BETWEEN WHAT LIFE PROMISES AND WHAT IT DELIVERS MOST KEENLY.
CO DENC
YOUTH REVOLT IS THE KEY TO SOCIAL REVOLT.
AND WHAT COULD BE MORE REVOLTING THAN THE ROCK 'N' ROLL?

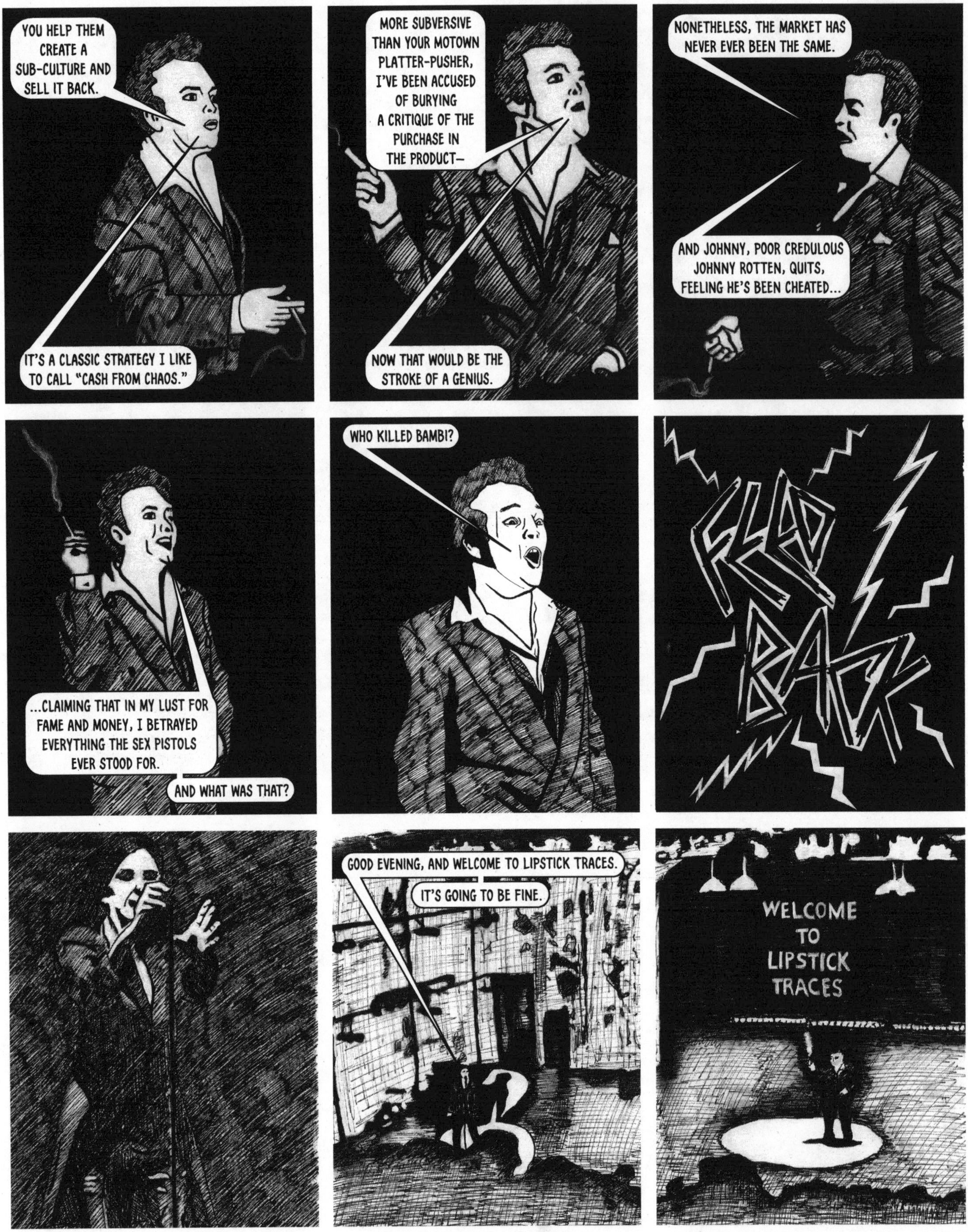
YOU HELP THEM CREATE A SUB-CULTURE AND SELL IT BACK.
IT'S A CLASSIC STRATEGY I LIKE TO CALL "CASH FROM CHAOS."
MORE SUBVERSIVE THAN YOUR MOTOWN PLATTER-PUSHER, I'VE BEEN ACCUSED OF BURYING A CRITIQUE OF THE PURCHASE IN THE PRODUCT—
NOW THAT WOULD BE THE STROKE OF A GENIUS.
NONETHELESS, THE MARKET HAS NEVER EVER BEEN THE SAME.
AND JOHNNY, POOR CREDULOUS JOHNNY ROTTEN, QUITS, FEELING HE'S BEEN CHEATED...
...CLAIMING THAT IN MY LUST FOR FAME AND MONEY, I BETRAYED EVERYTHING THE SEX PISTOLS EVER STOOD FOR.
AND WHAT WAS THAT?
WHO KILLED BAMBI?
GOOD EVENING, AND WELCOME TO LIPSTICK TRACES.
IT'S GOING TO BE FINE.
WELCOME TO LIPSTICK TRACES

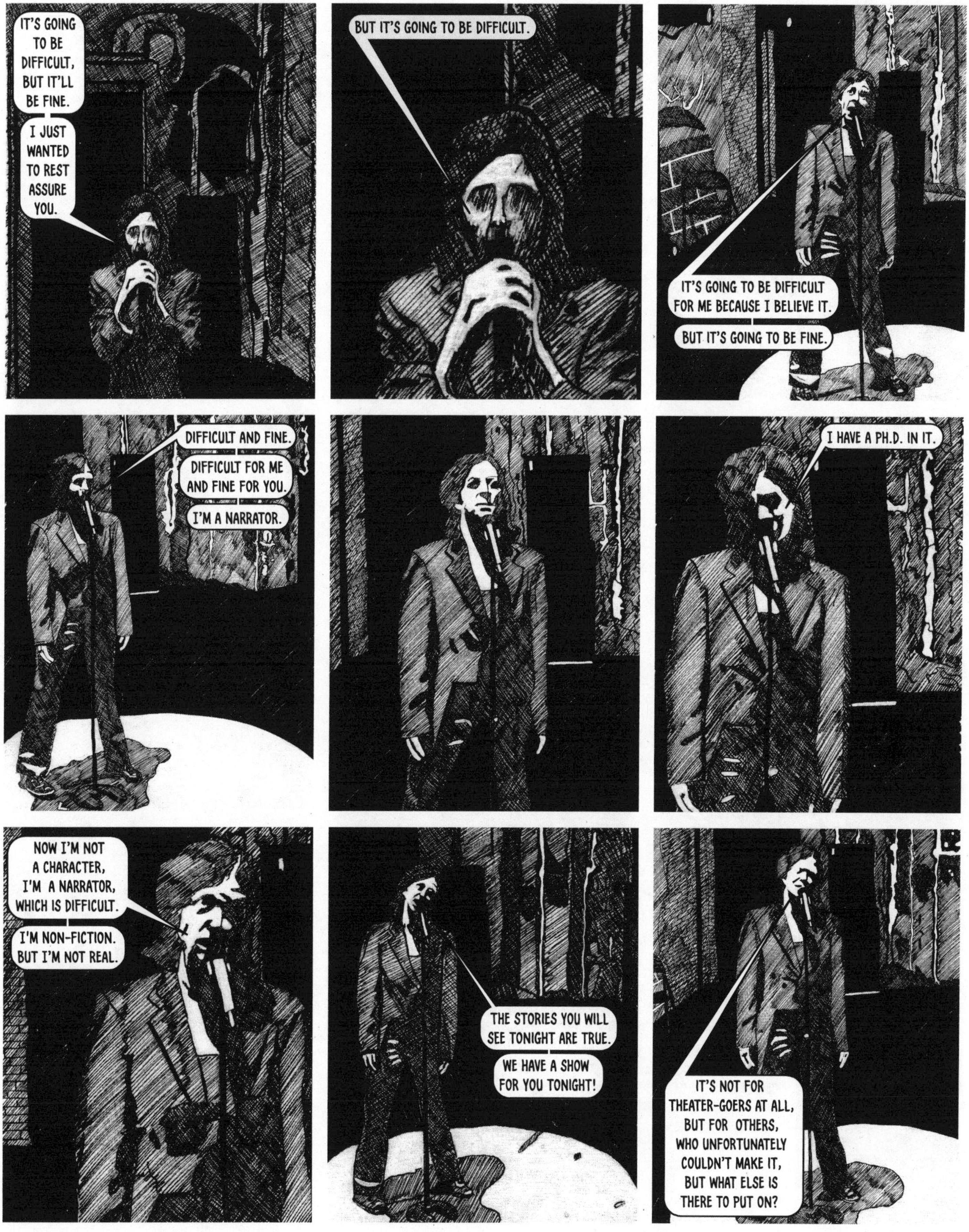
IT'S GOING TO BE DIFFICULT, BUT IT'LL BE FINE.
I JUST WANTED TO REST ASSURE YOU.
BUT IT'S GOING TO BE DIFFICULT.
IT'S GOING TO BE DIFFICULT FOR ME BECAUSE I BELIEVE IT.
BUT IT'S GOING TO BE FINE.
DIFFICULT AND FINE.
DIFFICULT FOR ME AND FINE FOR YOU.
I'M A NARRATOR.
I HAVE A PH.D. IN IT.
NOW I'M NOT A CHARACTER, I'M A NARRATOR, WHICH IS DIFFICULT.
I'M NON-FICTION. BUT I'M NOT REAL.
THE STORIES YOU WILL SEE TONIGHT ARE TRUE.
WE HAVE A SHOW FOR YOU TONIGHT!
IT'S NOT FOR THEATER-GOERS AT ALL, BUT FOR OTHERS, WHO UNFORTUNATELY COULDN'T MAKE IT, BUT WHAT ELSE IS THERE TO PUT ON?

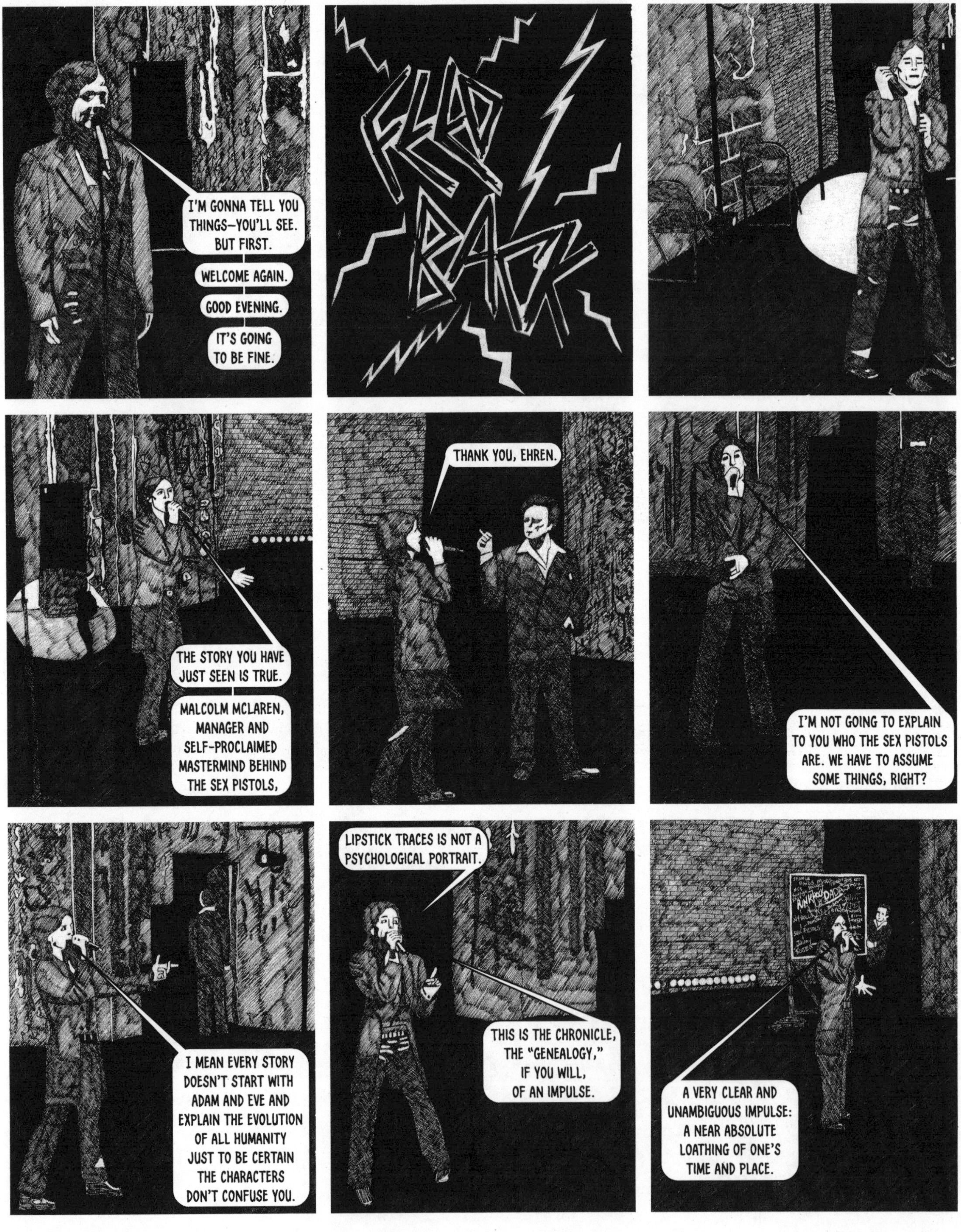
I'M GONNA TELL YOU THINGS—YOU'LL SEE. BUT FIRST.
WELCOME AGAIN.
GOOD EVENING.
IT'S GOING TO BE FINE.
THE STORY YOU HAVE JUST SEEN IS TRUE.
MALCOLM MCLAREN, MANAGER AND SELF-PROCLAIMED MASTERMIND BEHIND THE SEX PISTOLS,
THANK YOU, EHREN.
I'M NOT GOING TO EXPLAIN TO YOU WHO THE SEX PISTOLS ARE. WE HAVE TO ASSUME SOME THINGS, RIGHT?
I MEAN EVERY STORY DOESN'T START WITH ADAM AND EVE AND EXPLAIN THE EVOLUTION OF ALL HUMANITY JUST TO BE CERTAIN THE CHARACTERS DON'T CONFUSE YOU.
LIPSTICK TRACES IS NOT A PSYCHOLOGICAL PORTRAIT.
THIS IS THE CHRONICLE, THE "GENEALOGY," IF YOU WILL, OF AN IMPULSE.
A VERY CLEAR AND UNAMBIGUOUS IMPULSE: A NEAR ABSOLUTE LOATHING OF ONE'S TIME AND PLACE.

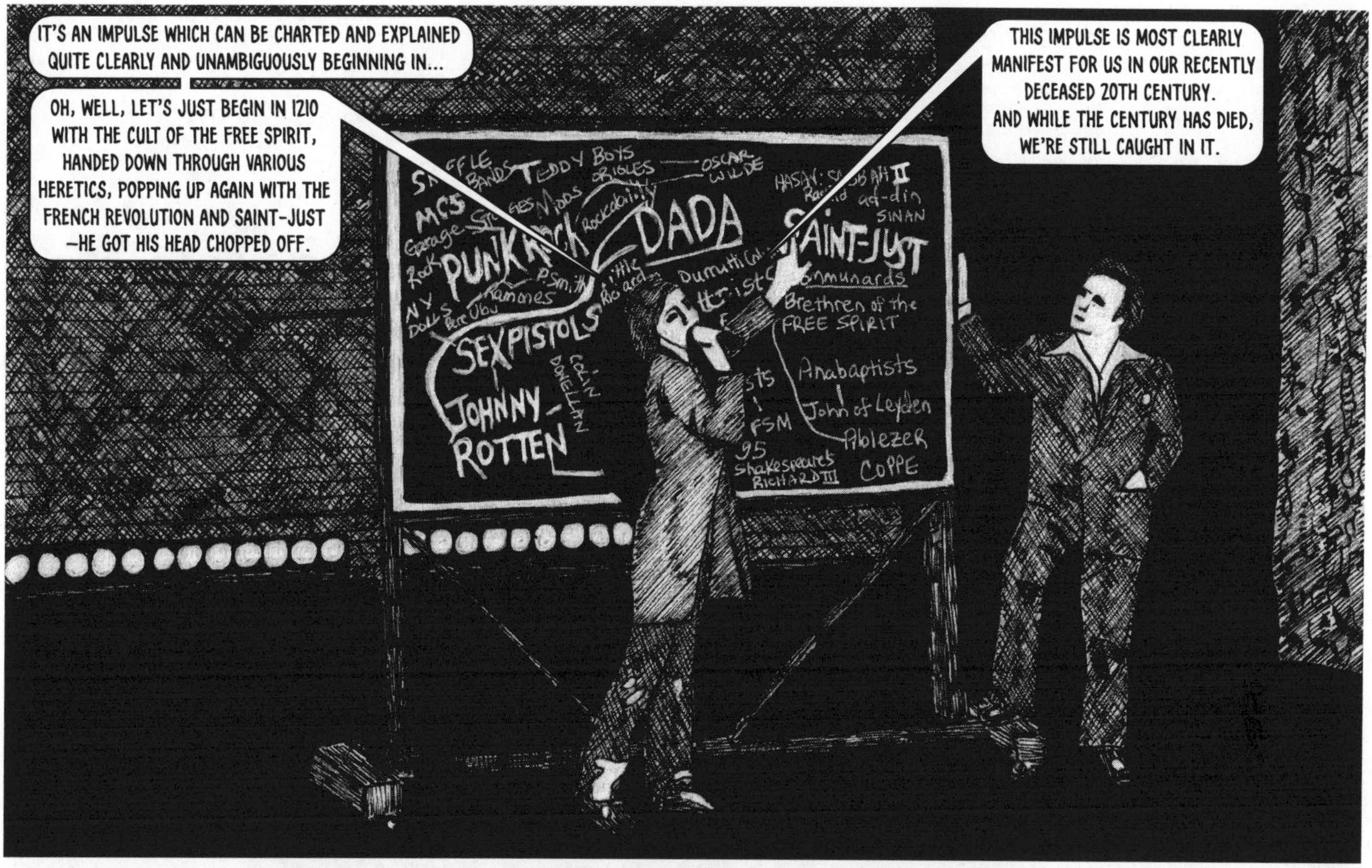
IT'S AN IMPULSE WHICH CAN BE CHARTED AND EXPLAINED QUITE CLEARLY AND UNAMBIGUOUSLY BEGINNING IN...
OH, WELL, LET'S JUST BEGIN IN 1210 WITH THE CULT OF THE FREE SPIRIT, HANDED DOWN THROUGH VARIOUS HERETICS, POPPING UP AGAIN WITH THE FRENCH REVOLUTION AND SAINT-JUST —HE GOT HIS HEAD CHOPPED OFF.
THIS IMPULSE IS MOST CLEARLY MANIFEST FOR US IN OUR RECENTLY DECEASED 20TH CENTURY. AND WHILE THE CENTURY HAS DIED, WE'RE STILL CAUGHT IN IT.

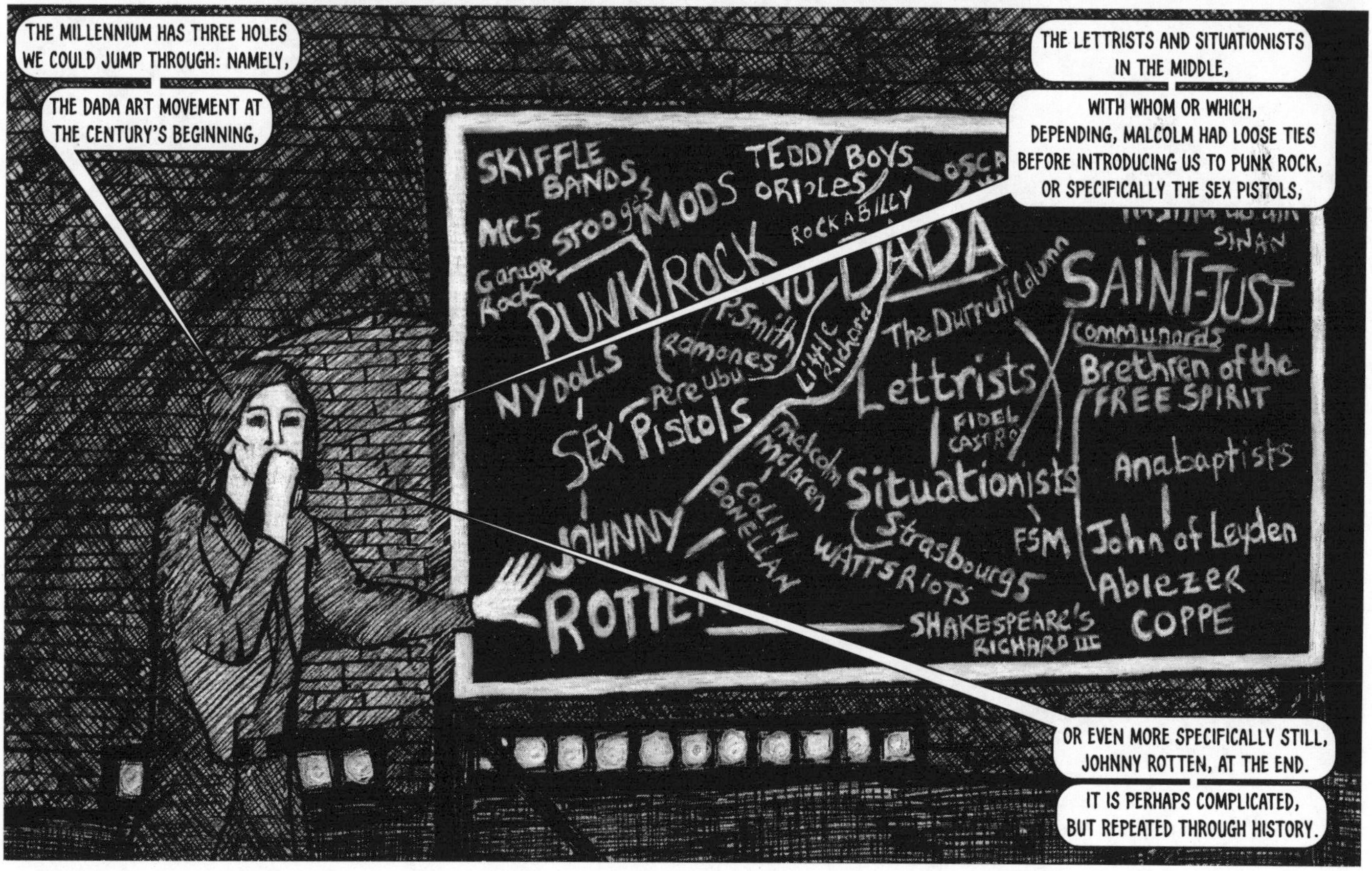
THE MILLENNIUM HAS THREE HOLES WE COULD JUMP THROUGH: NAMELY,
THE DADA ART MOVEMENT AT THE CENTURY'S BEGINNING,
THE LETTRISTS AND SITUATIONISTS IN THE MIDDLE,
WITH WHOM OR WHICH, DEPENDING, MALCOLM HAD LOOSE TIES BEFORE INTRODUCING US TO PUNK ROCK, OR SPECIFICALLY THE SEX PISTOLS,
OR EVEN MORE SPECIFICALLY STILL, JOHNNY ROTTEN, AT THE END.
IT IS PERHAPS COMPLICATED, BUT REPEATED THROUGH HISTORY.

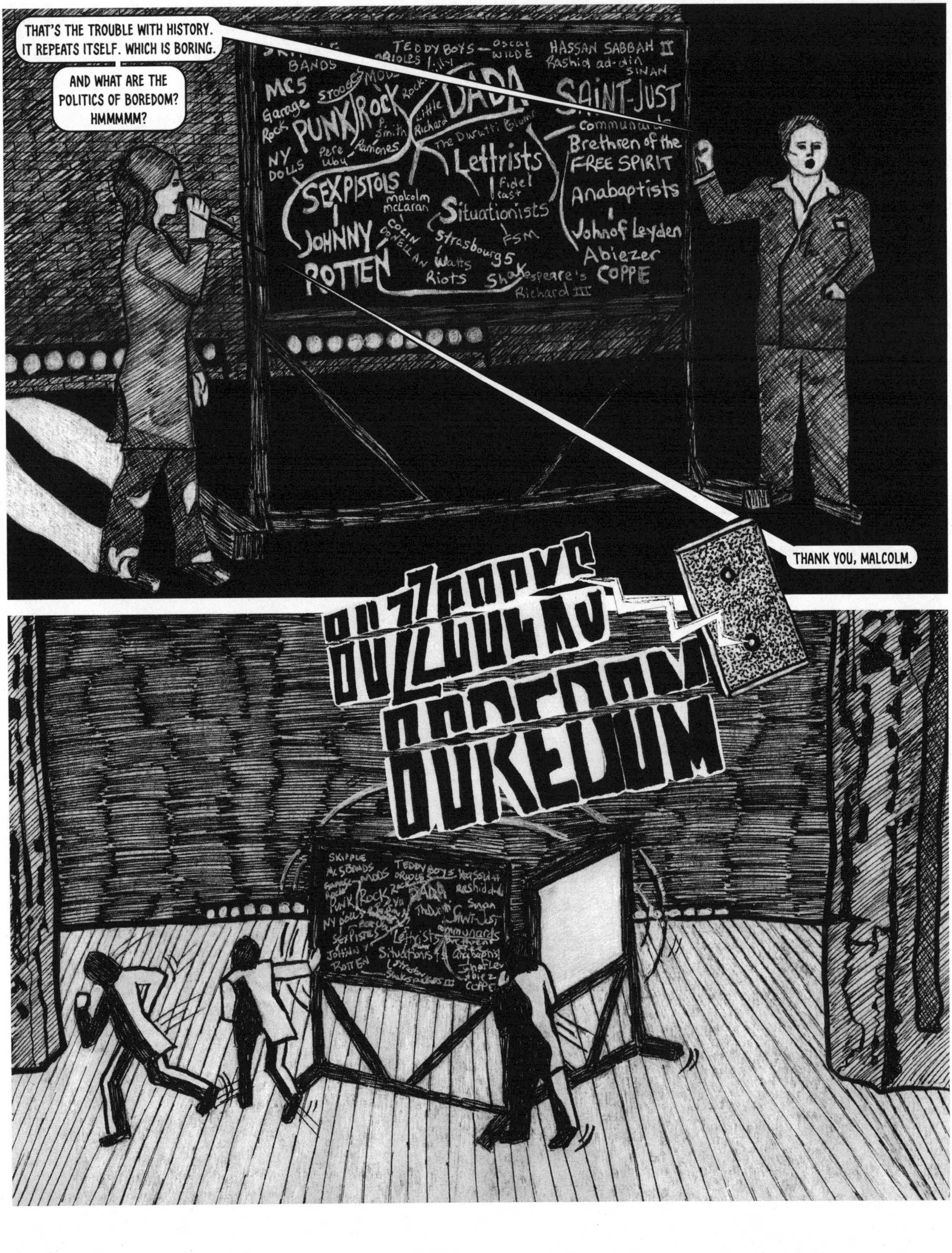

THAT'S THE TROUBLE WITH HISTORY. IT REPEATS ITSELF. WHICH IS BORING.
AND WHAT ARE THE POLITICS OF BOREDOM? HMMMMM?
BANDS
TEDDY BOYS — Oscar WILDE
ORIOLES
HASSAN SABBAH II
Rashid ad-din SINAN
MC5
STOOGES
MODS
Garage Rock
PUNK ROCK
Rock
Little Richard
DADA
SAINT-JUST
communards
P. Smith
The Durutti Column
NY DOLLS
Pere Ubu
Ramones
Lettrists
Brethren of the FREE SPIRIT
SEXPISTOLS
malcolm mcLaran
Fidel cast
Situationists
Anabaptists
JOHNNY ROTTEN
COLIN DONELLAN
Strasbourg 5
FSM
John of Leyden
Watts Riots
Shakespeare's Richard III
Abiezer COPPE
THANK YOU, MALCOLM.
BOREDOM

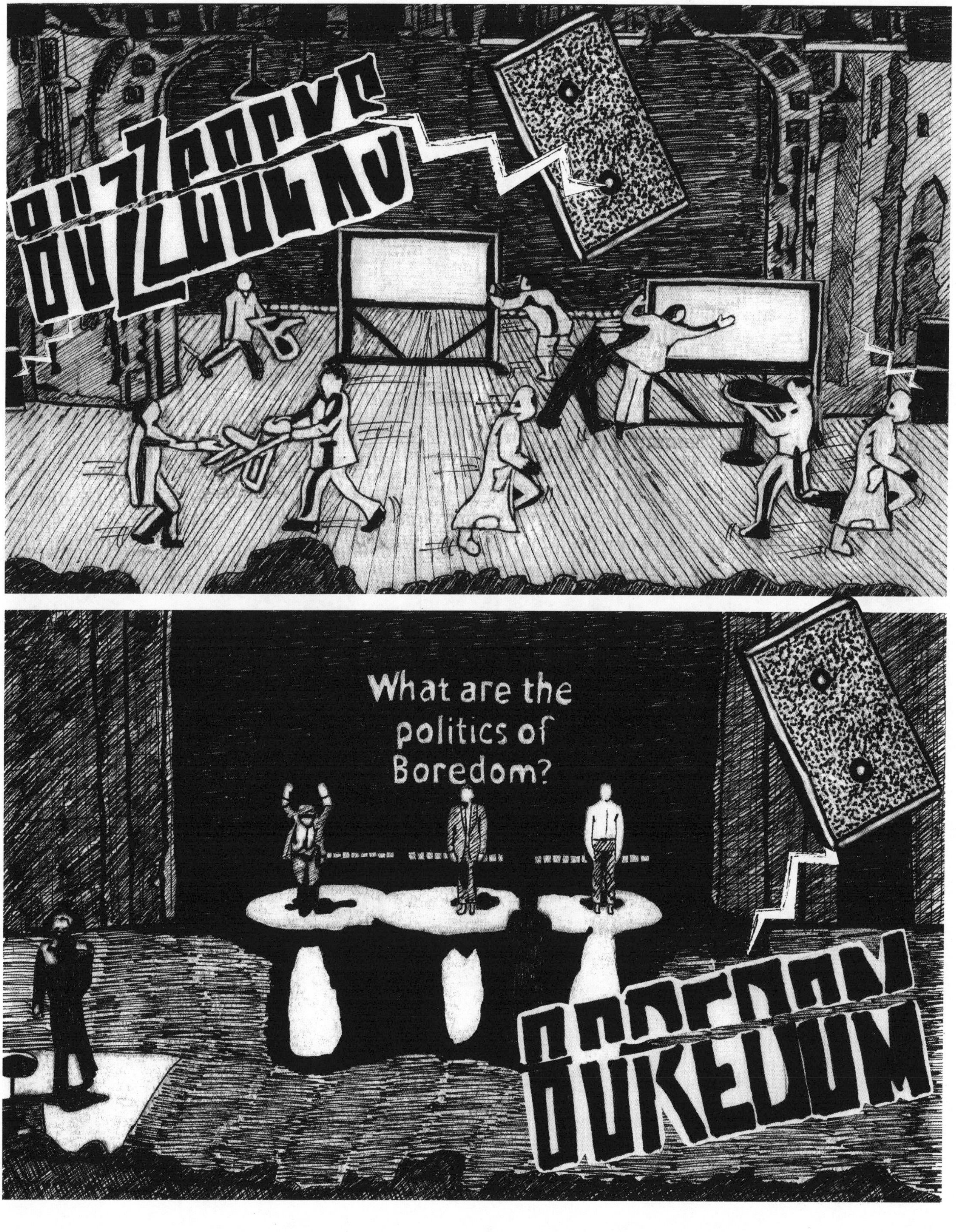
BUZZWORDS
What are the politics of Boredom?
BOREDOM

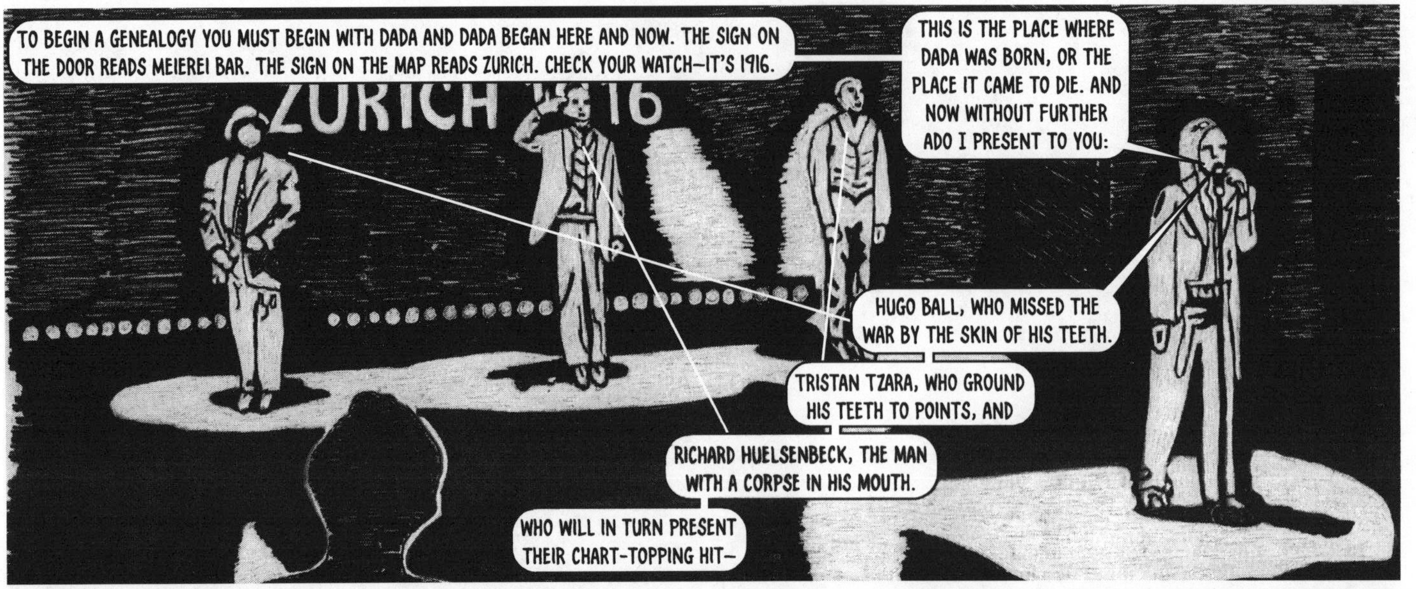
TO BEGIN A GENEALOGY YOU MUST BEGIN WITH DADA AND DADA BEGAN HERE AND NOW. THE SIGN ON THE DOOR READS MEIEREI BAR. THE SIGN ON THE MAP READS ZURICH. CHECK YOUR WATCH—IT'S 1916.
THIS IS THE PLACE WHERE DADA WAS BORN, OR THE PLACE IT CAME TO DIE. AND NOW WITHOUT FURTHER ADO I PRESENT TO YOU:
HUGO BALL, WHO MISSED THE WAR BY THE SKIN OF HIS TEETH.
TRISTAN TZARA, WHO GROUND HIS TEETH TO POINTS, AND
RICHARD HUELSENBECK, THE MAN WITH A CORPSE IN HIS MOUTH.
WHO WILL IN TURN PRESENT THEIR CHART-TOPPING HIT—
ZURICH 1916

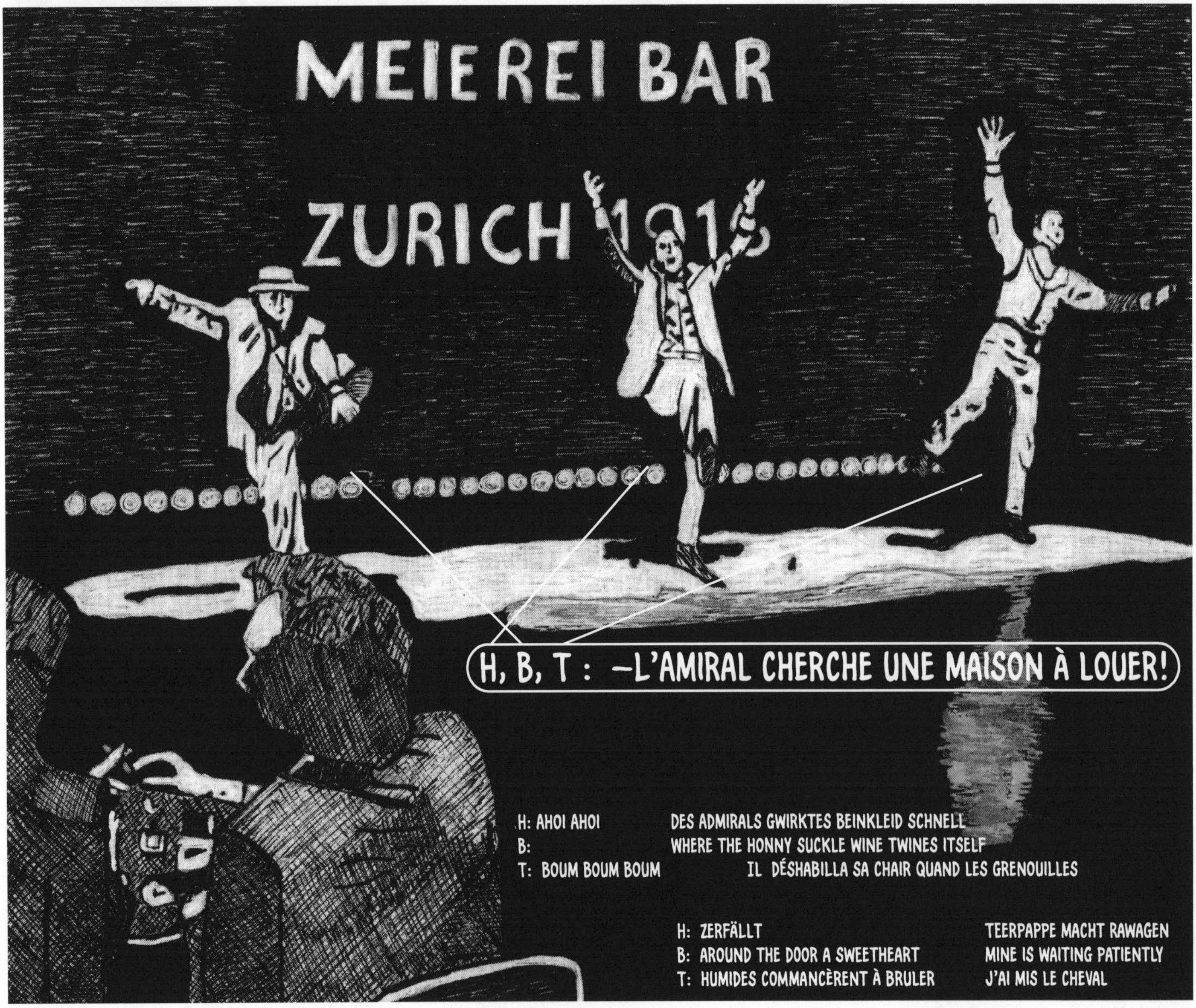
MEIEREI BAR
ZURICH 1916
H, B, T : —L'AMIRAL CHERCHE UNE MAISON À LOUER!
H: AHOI AHOI DES ADMIRALS GWIRKTES BEINKLEID SCHNELL
B: WHERE THE HONNY SUCKLE WINE TWINES ITSELF
T: BOUM BOUM BOUM IL DÉSHABILLA SA CHAIR QUAND LES GRENOUILLES
H: ZERFÄLLT TEERPAPPE MACHT RAWAGEN
B: AROUND THE DOOR A SWEETHEART MINE IS WAITING PATIENTLY
T: HUMIDES COMMANCÈRENT À BRULER J'AI MIS LE CHEVAL

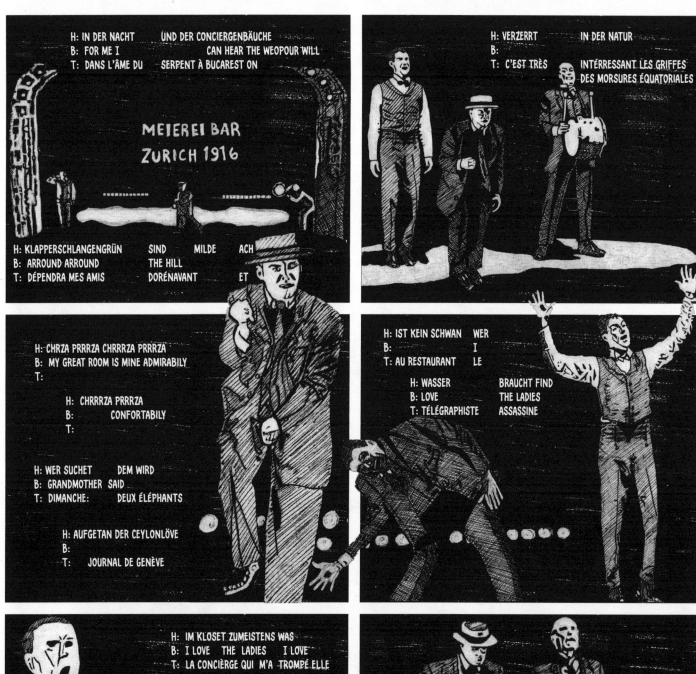

H: IN DER NACHT   ÜND DER CONCIERGENBÄUCHE
B: FOR ME I   CAN HEAR THE WEOPOUR WILL
T: DANS L'ÂME DU   SERPENT À BUCAREST ON

MEIEREI BAR
ZURICH 1916

H: KLAPPERSCHLANGENGRÜN   SIND   MILDE   ACH
B: ARROUND ARROUND   THE HILL
T: DÉPENDRA MES AMIS   DORÉNAVANT   ET

H: VERZERRT   IN DER NATUR
B:
T: C'EST TRÈS   INTÉRRESSANT LES GRIFFES
               DES MORSURES ÉQUATORIALES

H: CHRZA PRRRZA CHRRRZA PRRRZA
B: MY GREAT ROOM IS MINE ADMIRABILY
T:

    H: CHRRRZA PRRRZA
    B: CONFORTABILY
    T:

H: WER SUCHET   DEM WIRD
B: GRANDMOTHER SAID
T: DIMANCHE: DEUX ÉLÉPHANTS

    H: AUFGETAN DER CEYLONLÖVE
    B:
    T: JOURNAL DE GENÈVE

H: IST KEIN SCHWAN   WER
B: I
T: AU RESTAURANT   LE

    H: WASSER   BRAUCHT FIND
    B: LOVE   THE LADIES
    T: TÉLÉGRAPHISTE ASSASSINE

H: IM KLOSET ZUMEISTENS WAS
B: I LOVE THE LADIES   I LOVE
T: LA CONCIÈRGE QUI M'A TROMPÉ ELLE

    H: ER   NÖTIG   HÄTT AHOI
    B: TO   BE AMONG THE GIRLS
    T: A   VENDU L'APPARTEMENT

H: IUCHÉ AHOI   IUCHÉ
B:
T: QUE J'AVAIS LOUÉ DAN L'ÉGLISE APRÈS LA MESSE LE PÊCHEUR
                               DIT À LA COMTESSE:

H: FIND WAS ER NÖTIG HÄTT   O SÜSS GEQUOLLNES
B: AND WHEN IT'S FIVE O'CLOCK   AND TEA IS SET I LIKE
T: ADIEU MATHILDE   LE TRAIN TRAINE LA

H: STELLDICHEIN DES ADMIRALS IM ABENDSCHEIN URU URU
B: TO HAVE MY TEA WITH SOME BRUNET SHAI SHAI
T: FUMÉE COMME LA FUITE DE L'ANIMAL BLESSÉ AUX
H: URO URU URU URO URU URU URU URO
B: SHAI SHAI SHAI SHAI SHAI EVERY BODY IS
T: INTESTINS ECRASÉS
H: PATACLAN PATABLAN PATAPLAN URI URI URO
B: IS DOING IT DOING IT DOING IT EVERY BODY IS
T:
H: IN JOSCHIWARA DRÖHNT DER BRAND UND KNALLT MIT
B: DOING IT DOING IT
T: TANDIS QUE LES ARCHANGES TOMBENT
H:
B: OH
T: OH! MON CHER C'EST SI DIFFICILE
H: PEITSCHEN UM DIE LENDEN
B: OH YES YES YES YES YES YES
T: LA RUE S'ENFUIT AVEC MON BAGGAGE
H: IM CHLAFSACK
B: YES YES
T: À TRAVES LA VILLE
H: GRÖHLT DER ALTE
B: YES YES YES
T: UN MÉTRO MÊLE SON
H: OBERPRIESTER UND
B: OH YES OH YES OH YES
T: CINÉMA LA PRORE
H: ZIEGT DER
B: OH YES YES
T: DE JE VOUS ADORE
H: SCHENKEL VOLLE TASTATUR
B: YES OH YES SIR
T: ETAIT AU CASINO DU SYCOMORE

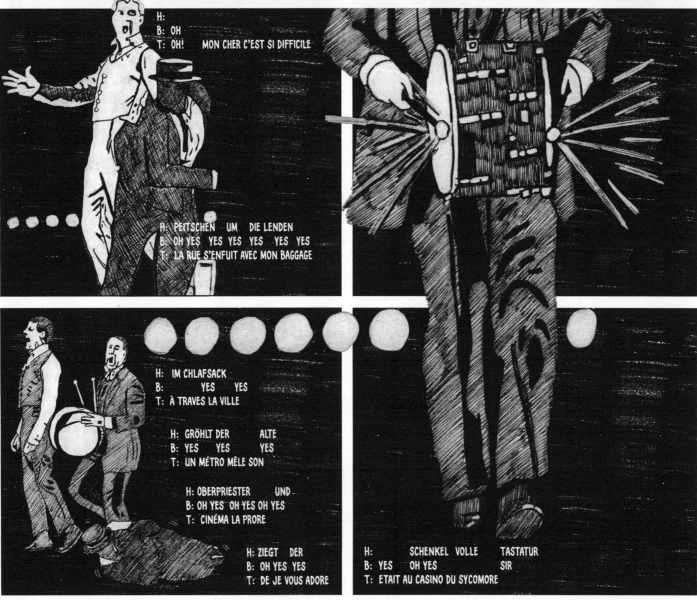

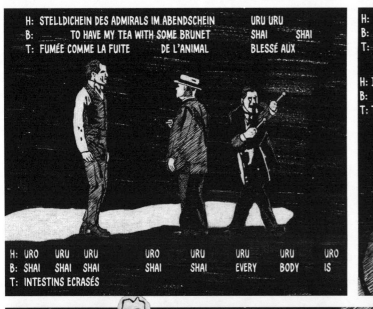

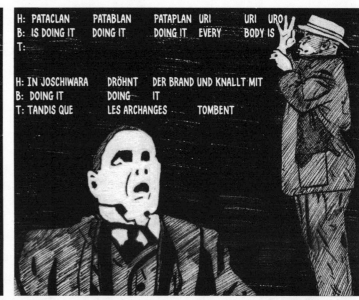

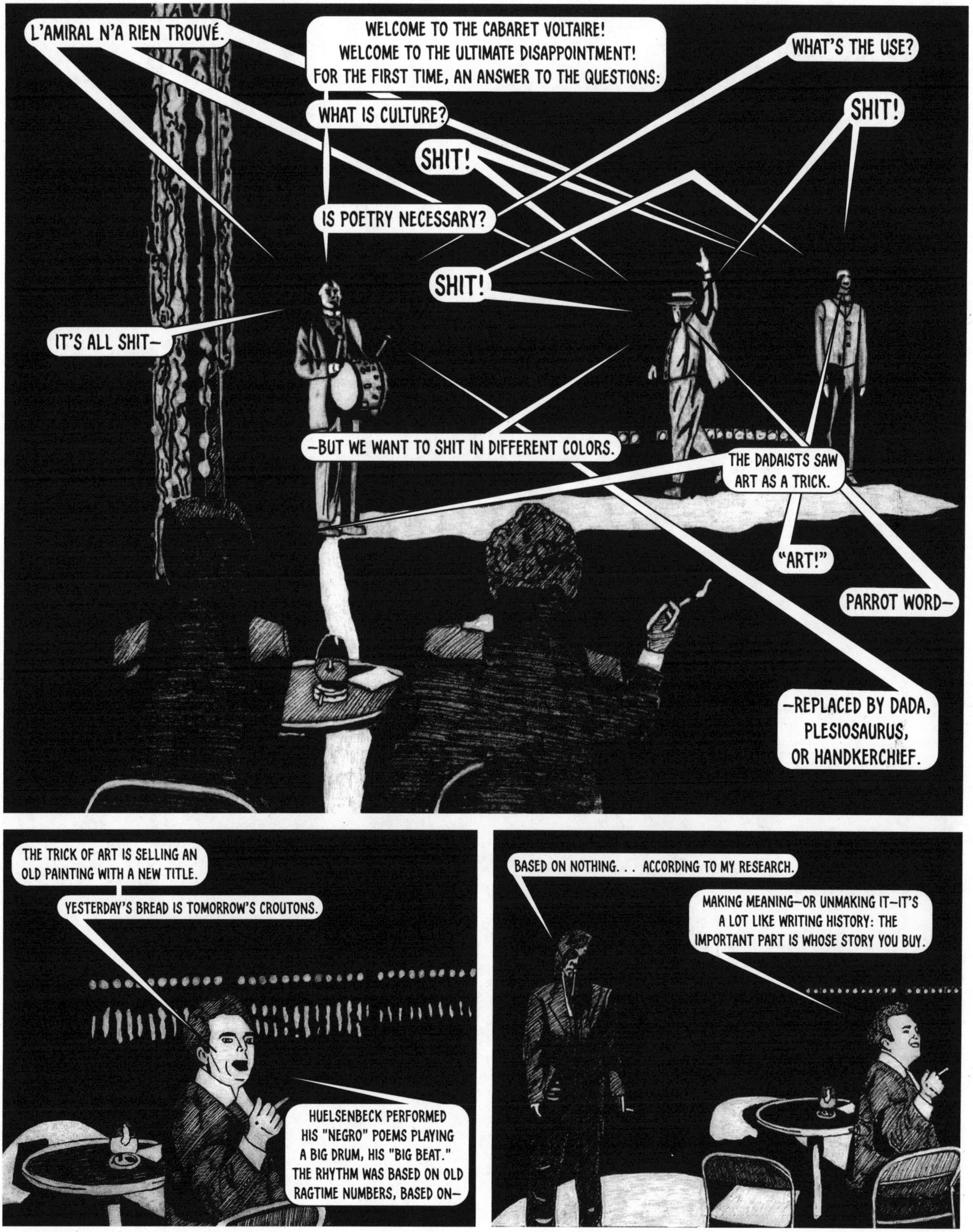
L'AMIRAL N'A RIEN TROUVÉ.
WELCOME TO THE CABARET VOLTAIRE! WELCOME TO THE ULTIMATE DISAPPOINTMENT! FOR THE FIRST TIME, AN ANSWER TO THE QUESTIONS:
WHAT'S THE USE?
WHAT IS CULTURE?
SHIT!
SHIT!
IS POETRY NECESSARY?
SHIT!
IT'S ALL SHIT—
—BUT WE WANT TO SHIT IN DIFFERENT COLORS.
THE DADAISTS SAW ART AS A TRICK.
"ART!"
PARROT WORD—
—REPLACED BY DADA, PLESIOSAURUS, OR HANDKERCHIEF.
THE TRICK OF ART IS SELLING AN OLD PAINTING WITH A NEW TITLE.
YESTERDAY'S BREAD IS TOMORROW'S CROUTONS.
HUELSENBECK PERFORMED HIS "NEGRO" POEMS PLAYING A BIG DRUM, HIS "BIG BEAT." THE RHYTHM WAS BASED ON OLD RAGTIME NUMBERS, BASED ON—
BASED ON NOTHING. . . ACCORDING TO MY RESEARCH.
MAKING MEANING—OR UNMAKING IT—IT'S A LOT LIKE WRITING HISTORY: THE IMPORTANT PART IS WHOSE STORY YOU BUY.

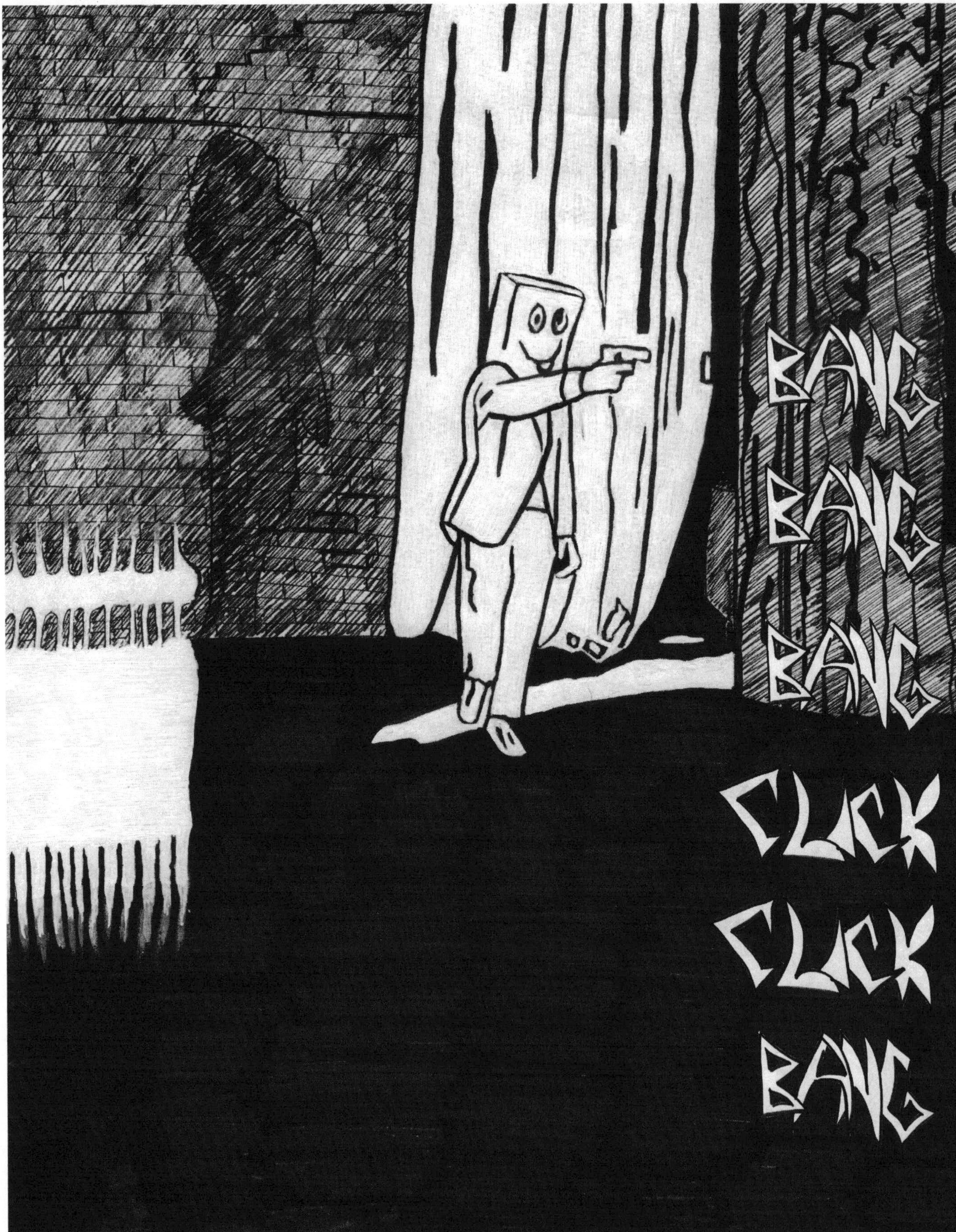
BANG
BANG
BANG
CLICK
CLICK
BANG

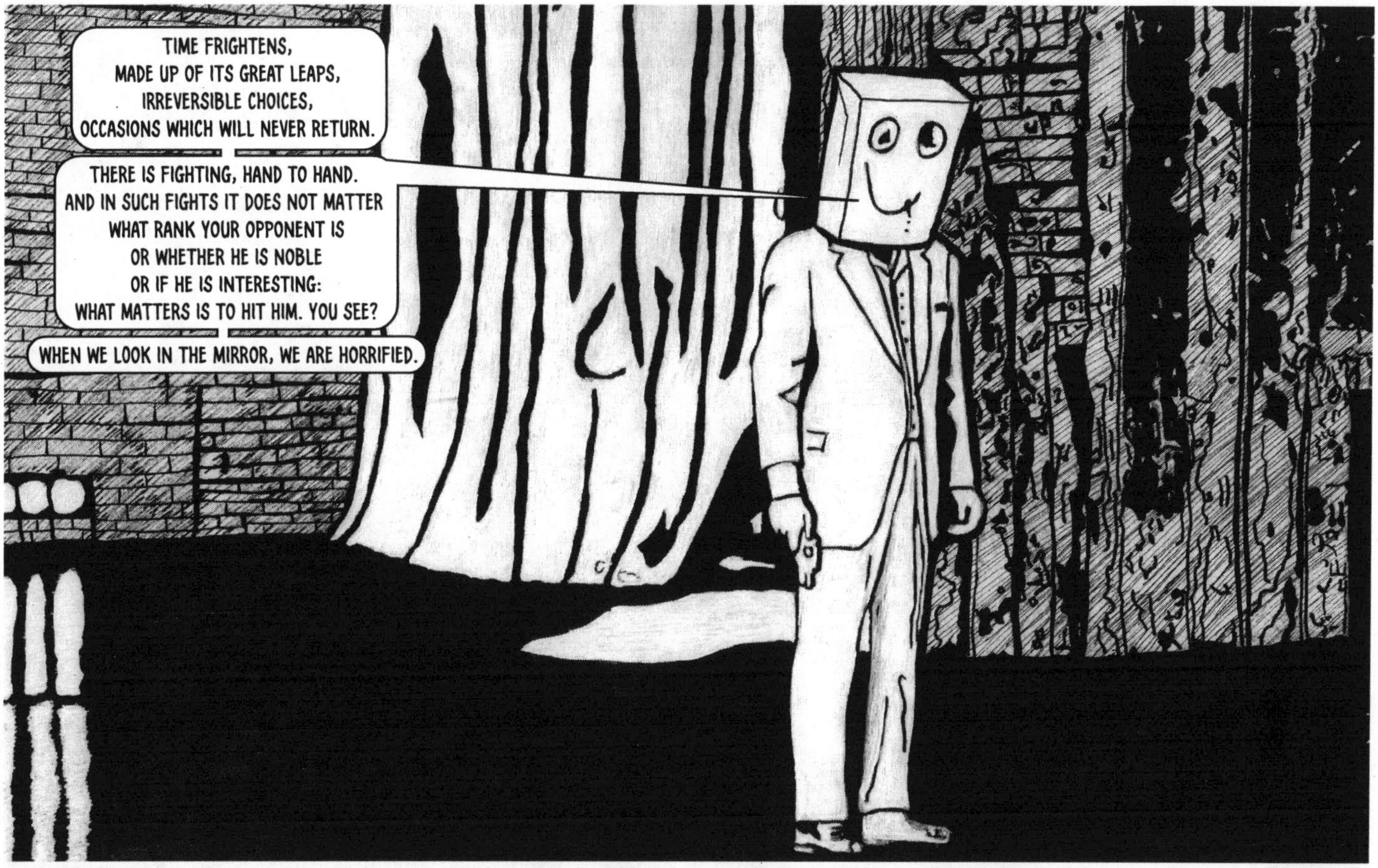
TIME FRIGHTENS,
MADE UP OF ITS GREAT LEAPS,
IRREVERSIBLE CHOICES,
OCCASIONS WHICH WILL NEVER RETURN.
THERE IS FIGHTING, HAND TO HAND.
AND IN SUCH FIGHTS IT DOES NOT MATTER
WHAT RANK YOUR OPPONENT IS
OR WHETHER HE IS NOBLE
OR IF HE IS INTERESTING:
WHAT MATTERS IS TO HIT HIM. YOU SEE?
WHEN WE LOOK IN THE MIRROR, WE ARE HORRIFIED.

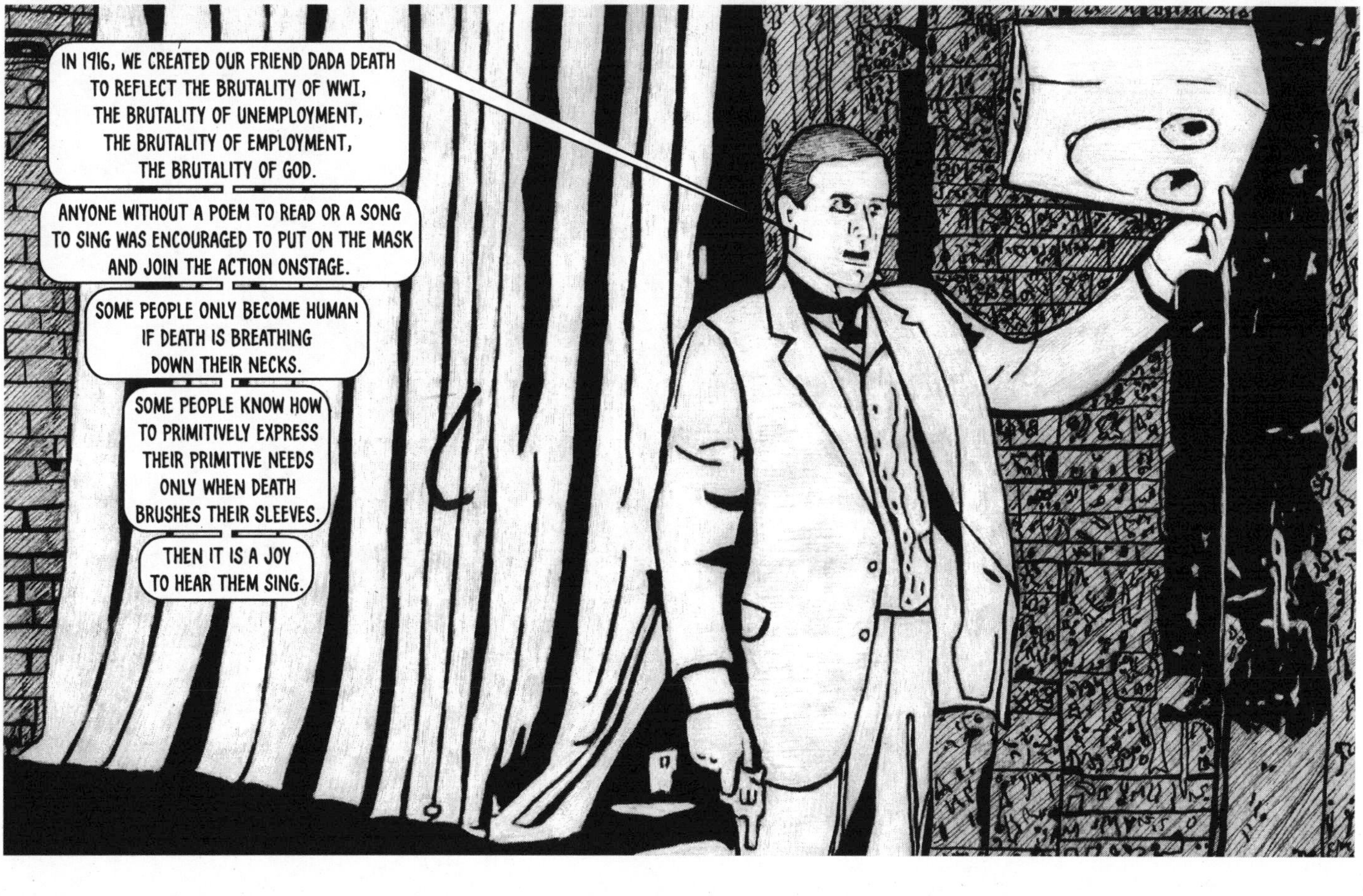
IN 1916, WE CREATED OUR FRIEND DADA DEATH
TO REFLECT THE BRUTALITY OF WWI,
THE BRUTALITY OF UNEMPLOYMENT,
THE BRUTALITY OF EMPLOYMENT,
THE BRUTALITY OF GOD.
ANYONE WITHOUT A POEM TO READ OR A SONG
TO SING WAS ENCOURAGED TO PUT ON THE MASK
AND JOIN THE ACTION ONSTAGE.
SOME PEOPLE ONLY BECOME HUMAN
IF DEATH IS BREATHING
DOWN THEIR NECKS.
SOME PEOPLE KNOW HOW
TO PRIMITIVELY EXPRESS
THEIR PRIMITIVE NEEDS
ONLY WHEN DEATH
BRUSHES THEIR SLEEVES.
THEN IT IS A JOY
TO HEAR THEM SING.

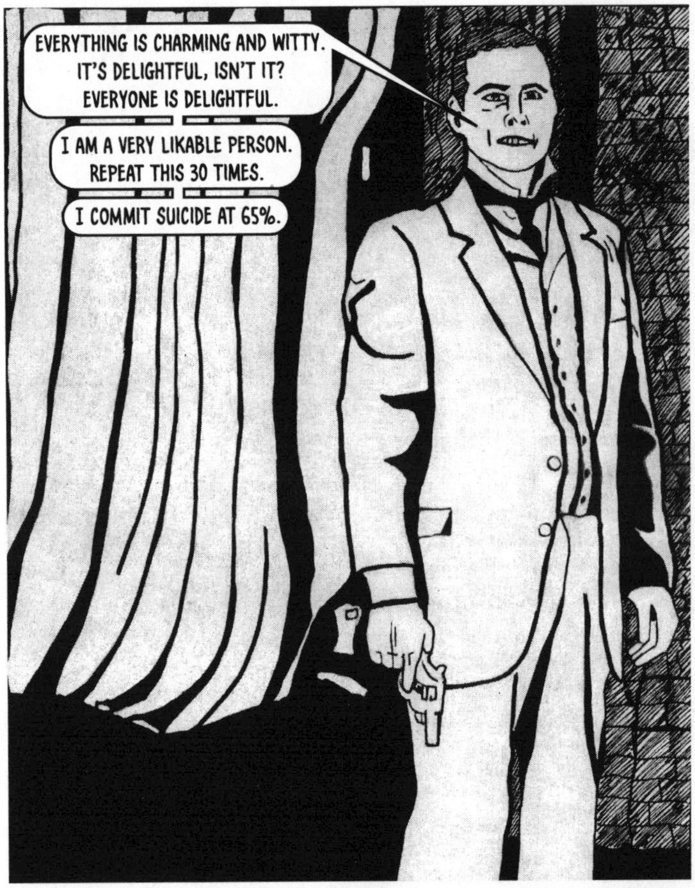
EVERYTHING IS CHARMING AND WITTY. IT'S DELIGHTFUL, ISN'T IT? EVERYONE IS DELIGHTFUL.
I AM A VERY LIKABLE PERSON. REPEAT THIS 30 TIMES.
I COMMIT SUICIDE AT 65%.

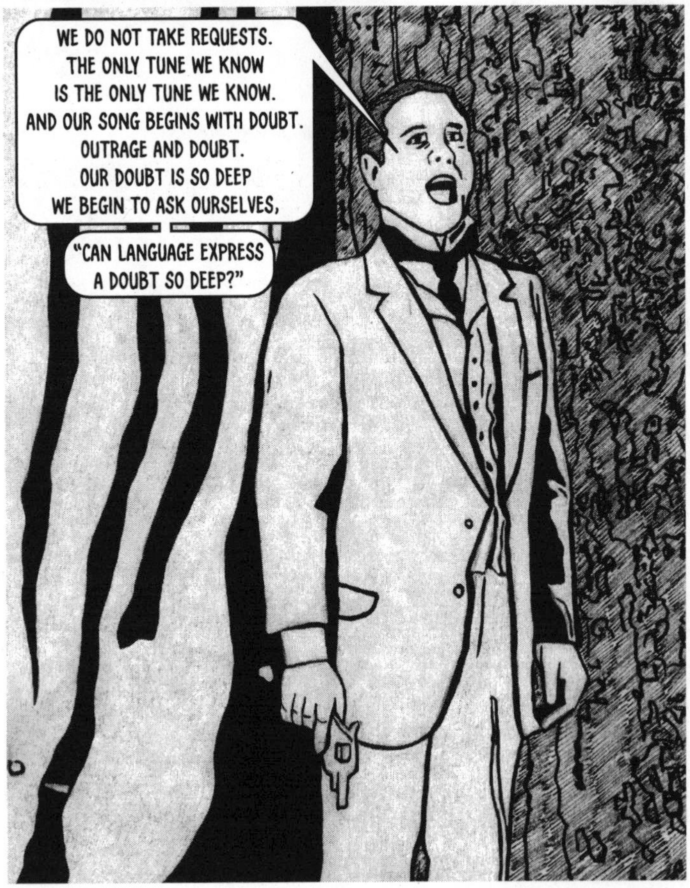
WE DO NOT TAKE REQUESTS. THE ONLY TUNE WE KNOW IS THE ONLY TUNE WE KNOW. AND OUR SONG BEGINS WITH DOUBT. OUTRAGE AND DOUBT. OUR DOUBT IS SO DEEP WE BEGIN TO ASK OURSELVES,
"CAN LANGUAGE EXPRESS A DOUBT SO DEEP?"

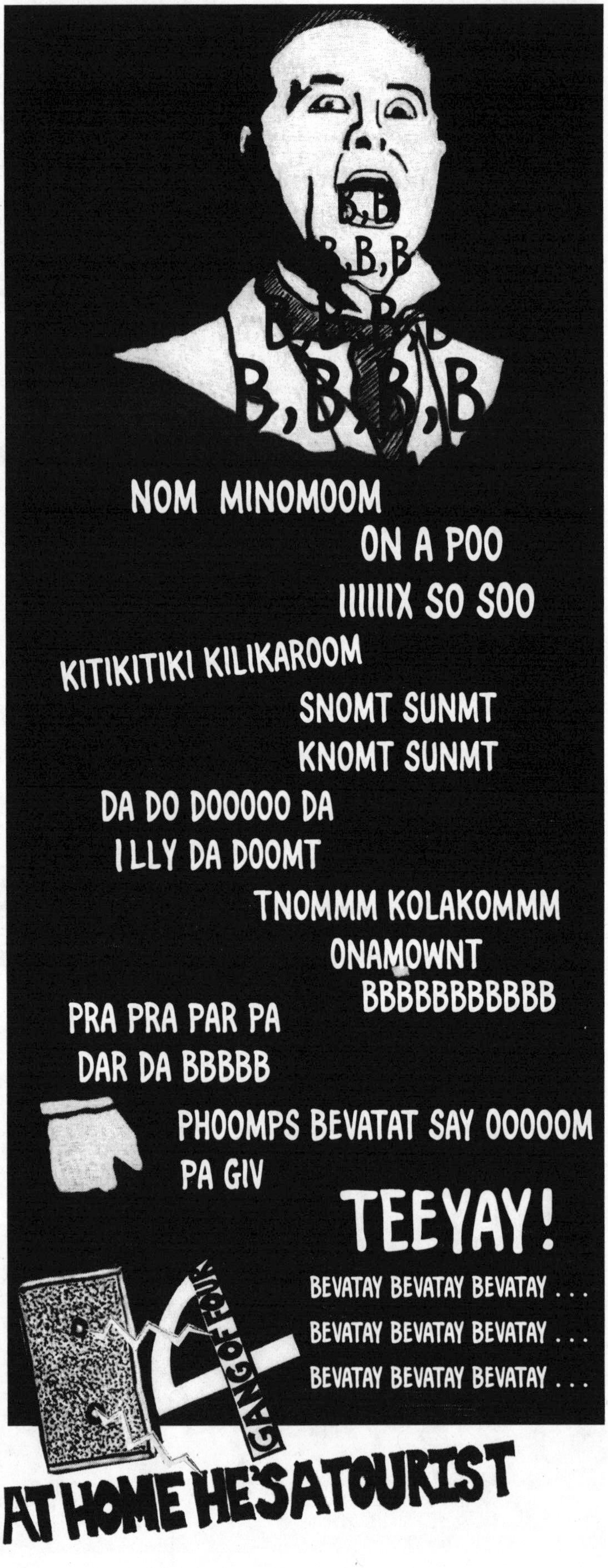
B,B
B,B,B
B,B,B,B
NOM MINOMOOM
ON A POO
IIIIIIX SO SOO
KITIKITIKI KILIKAROOM
SNOMT SUNMT
KNOMT SUNMT
DA DO DOOOOO DA
I LLY DA DOOMT
TNOMMM KOLAKOMMM
ONAMOWNT
BBBBBBBBBBB
PRA PRA PAR PA
DAR DA BBBBB
PHOOMPS BEVATAT SAY OOOOOM
PA GIV
TEEYAY!
BEVATAY BEVATAY BEVATAY . . .
BEVATAY BEVATAY BEVATAY . . .
BEVATAY BEVATAY BEVATAY . . .
GANG OF FOUR
AT HOME HE'S A TOURIST

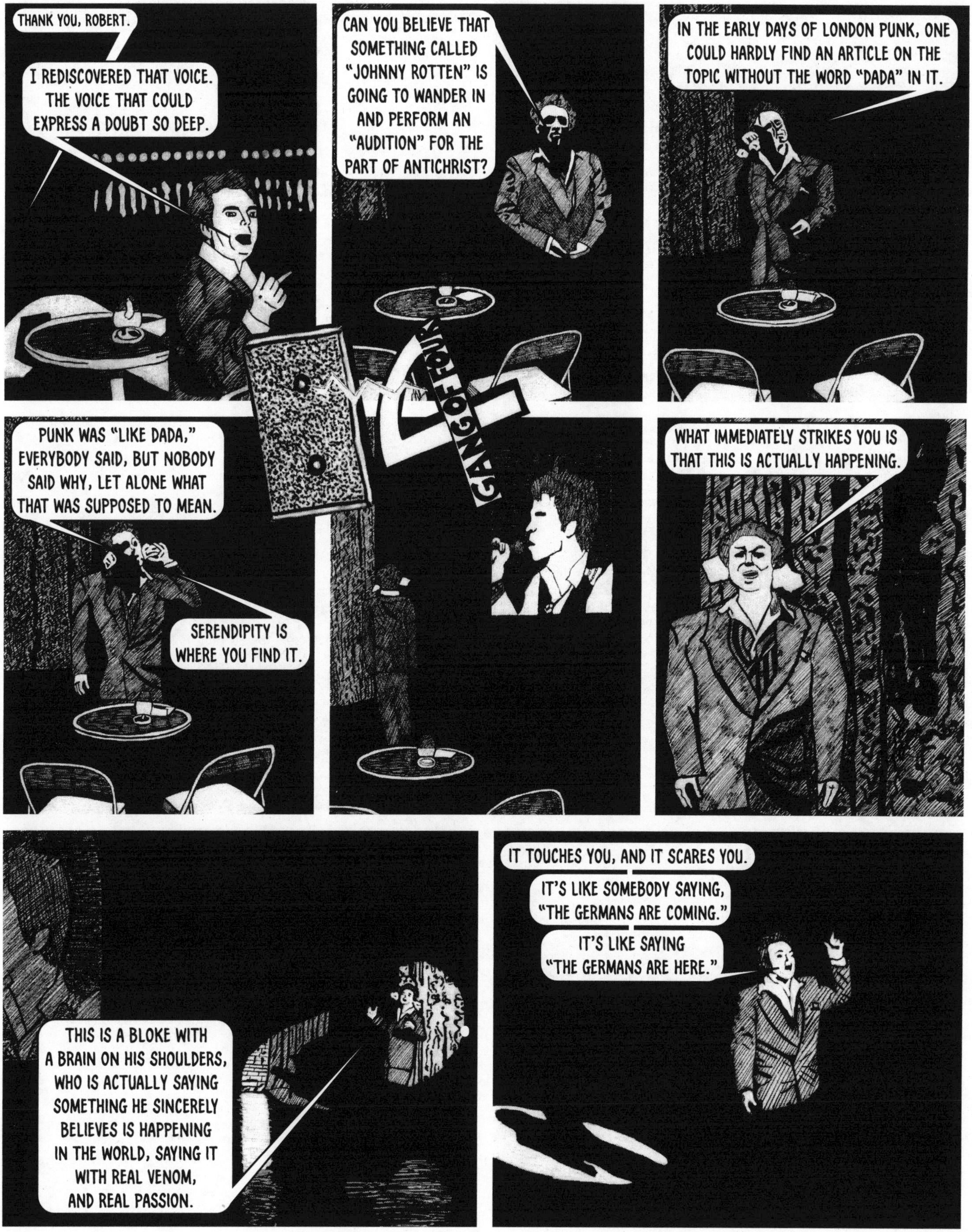
THANK YOU, ROBERT.
I REDISCOVERED THAT VOICE. THE VOICE THAT COULD EXPRESS A DOUBT SO DEEP.
CAN YOU BELIEVE THAT SOMETHING CALLED "JOHNNY ROTTEN" IS GOING TO WANDER IN AND PERFORM AN "AUDITION" FOR THE PART OF ANTICHRIST?
IN THE EARLY DAYS OF LONDON PUNK, ONE COULD HARDLY FIND AN ARTICLE ON THE TOPIC WITHOUT THE WORD "DADA" IN IT.
GANG OF FOUR
PUNK WAS "LIKE DADA," EVERYBODY SAID, BUT NOBODY SAID WHY, LET ALONE WHAT THAT WAS SUPPOSED TO MEAN.
SERENDIPITY IS WHERE YOU FIND IT.
WHAT IMMEDIATELY STRIKES YOU IS THAT THIS IS ACTUALLY HAPPENING.
THIS IS A BLOKE WITH A BRAIN ON HIS SHOULDERS, WHO IS ACTUALLY SAYING SOMETHING HE SINCERELY BELIEVES IS HAPPENING IN THE WORLD, SAYING IT WITH REAL VENOM, AND REAL PASSION.
IT TOUCHES YOU, AND IT SCARES YOU.
IT'S LIKE SOMEBODY SAYING, "THE GERMANS ARE COMING."
IT'S LIKE SAYING "THE GERMANS ARE HERE."

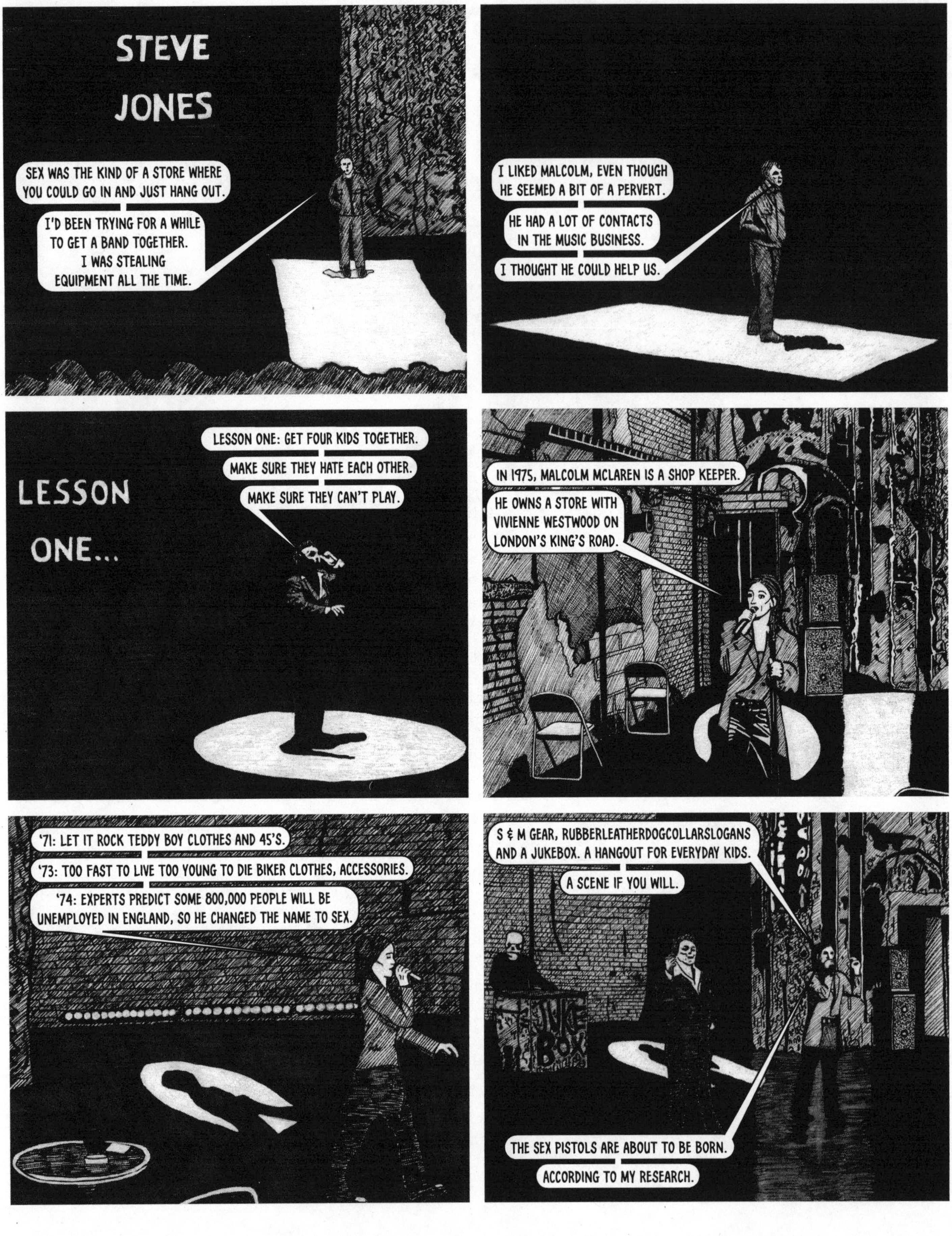
STEVE JONES
SEX WAS THE KIND OF A STORE WHERE YOU COULD GO IN AND JUST HANG OUT.
I'D BEEN TRYING FOR A WHILE TO GET A BAND TOGETHER. I WAS STEALING EQUIPMENT ALL THE TIME.
I LIKED MALCOLM, EVEN THOUGH HE SEEMED A BIT OF A PERVERT.
HE HAD A LOT OF CONTACTS IN THE MUSIC BUSINESS.
I THOUGHT HE COULD HELP US.
LESSON ONE...
LESSON ONE: GET FOUR KIDS TOGETHER.
MAKE SURE THEY HATE EACH OTHER.
MAKE SURE THEY CAN'T PLAY.
IN 1975, MALCOLM MCLAREN IS A SHOP KEEPER.
HE OWNS A STORE WITH VIVIENNE WESTWOOD ON LONDON'S KING'S ROAD.
'71: LET IT ROCK TEDDY BOY CLOTHES AND 45'S.
'73: TOO FAST TO LIVE TOO YOUNG TO DIE BIKER CLOTHES, ACCESSORIES.
'74: EXPERTS PREDICT SOME 800,000 PEOPLE WILL BE UNEMPLOYED IN ENGLAND, SO HE CHANGED THE NAME TO SEX.
S & M GEAR, RUBBERLEATHERDOGCOLLARSLOGANS AND A JUKEBOX. A HANGOUT FOR EVERYDAY KIDS.
A SCENE IF YOU WILL.
JUKE BOX
THE SEX PISTOLS ARE ABOUT TO BE BORN.
ACCORDING TO MY RESEARCH.

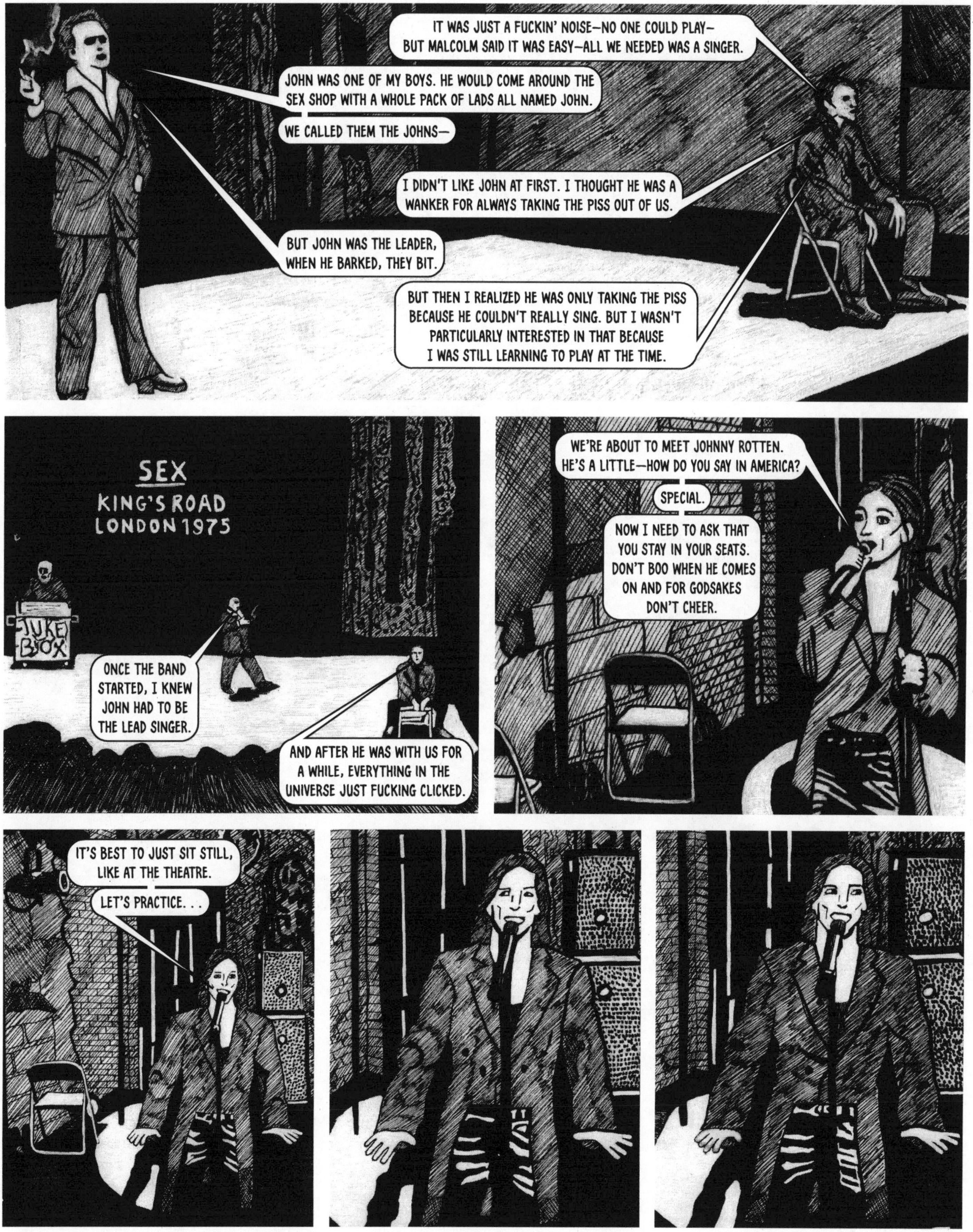
IT WAS JUST A FUCKIN' NOISE—NO ONE COULD PLAY—
BUT MALCOLM SAID IT WAS EASY—ALL WE NEEDED WAS A SINGER.
JOHN WAS ONE OF MY BOYS. HE WOULD COME AROUND THE SEX SHOP WITH A WHOLE PACK OF LADS ALL NAMED JOHN.
WE CALLED THEM THE JOHNS—
I DIDN'T LIKE JOHN AT FIRST. I THOUGHT HE WAS A WANKER FOR ALWAYS TAKING THE PISS OUT OF US.
BUT JOHN WAS THE LEADER, WHEN HE BARKED, THEY BIT.
BUT THEN I REALIZED HE WAS ONLY TAKING THE PISS BECAUSE HE COULDN'T REALLY SING. BUT I WASN'T PARTICULARLY INTERESTED IN THAT BECAUSE I WAS STILL LEARNING TO PLAY AT THE TIME.
SEX
KING'S ROAD
LONDON 1975
JUKE BOX
ONCE THE BAND STARTED, I KNEW JOHN HAD TO BE THE LEAD SINGER.
AND AFTER HE WAS WITH US FOR A WHILE, EVERYTHING IN THE UNIVERSE JUST FUCKING CLICKED.
WE'RE ABOUT TO MEET JOHNNY ROTTEN. HE'S A LITTLE—HOW DO YOU SAY IN AMERICA?
SPECIAL.
NOW I NEED TO ASK THAT YOU STAY IN YOUR SEATS. DON'T BOO WHEN HE COMES ON AND FOR GODSAKES DON'T CHEER.
IT'S BEST TO JUST SIT STILL, LIKE AT THE THEATRE.
LET'S PRACTICE. . .

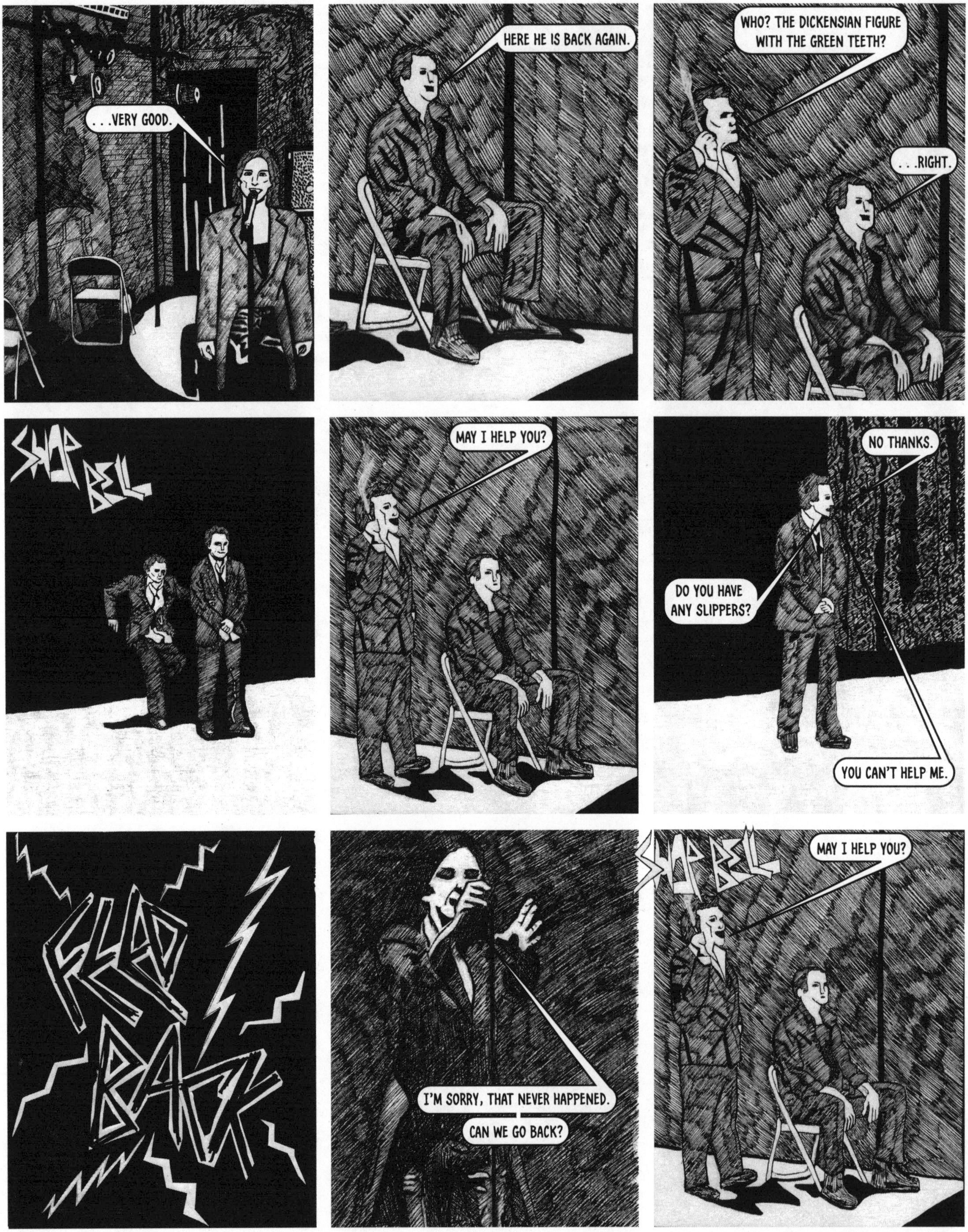
. . .VERY GOOD.
HERE HE IS BACK AGAIN.
WHO? THE DICKENSIAN FIGURE WITH THE GREEN TEETH?
. . .RIGHT.
SHOP BELL
MAY I HELP YOU?
NO THANKS.
DO YOU HAVE ANY SLIPPERS?
YOU CAN'T HELP ME.
FEED BACK
I'M SORRY, THAT NEVER HAPPENED.
CAN WE GO BACK?
SHOP BELL
MAY I HELP YOU?

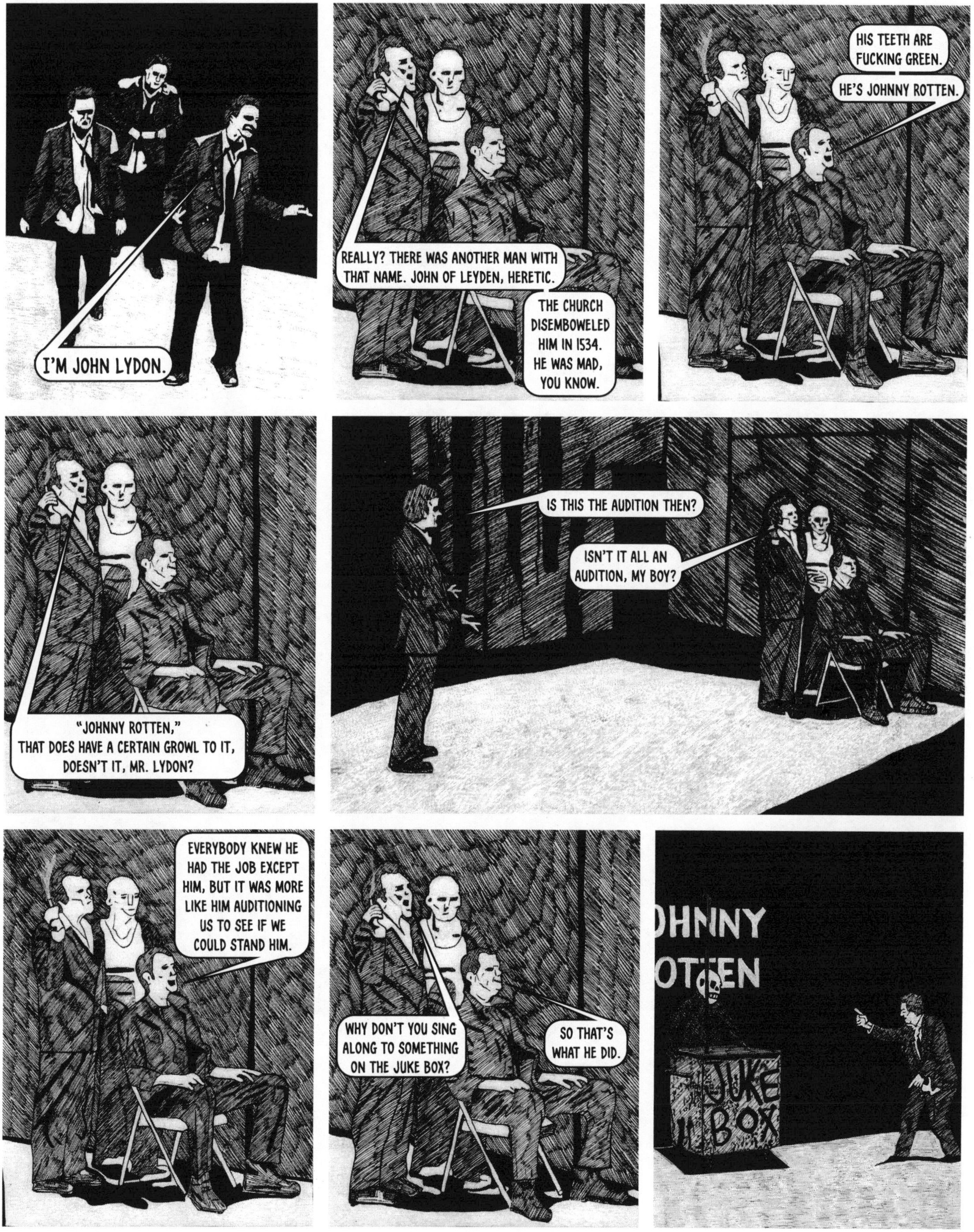
I'M JOHN LYDON.
REALLY? THERE WAS ANOTHER MAN WITH THAT NAME. JOHN OF LEYDEN, HERETIC.
THE CHURCH DISEMBOWELED HIM IN 1534. HE WAS MAD, YOU KNOW.
HIS TEETH ARE FUCKING GREEN.
HE'S JOHNNY ROTTEN.
"JOHNNY ROTTEN," THAT DOES HAVE A CERTAIN GROWL TO IT, DOESN'T IT, MR. LYDON?
IS THIS THE AUDITION THEN?
ISN'T IT ALL AN AUDITION, MY BOY?
EVERYBODY KNEW HE HAD THE JOB EXCEPT HIM, BUT IT WAS MORE LIKE HIM AUDITIONING US TO SEE IF WE COULD STAND HIM.
WHY DON'T YOU SING ALONG TO SOMETHING ON THE JUKE BOX?
SO THAT'S WHAT HE DID.
OHNNY
OTTEN
JUKE BOX

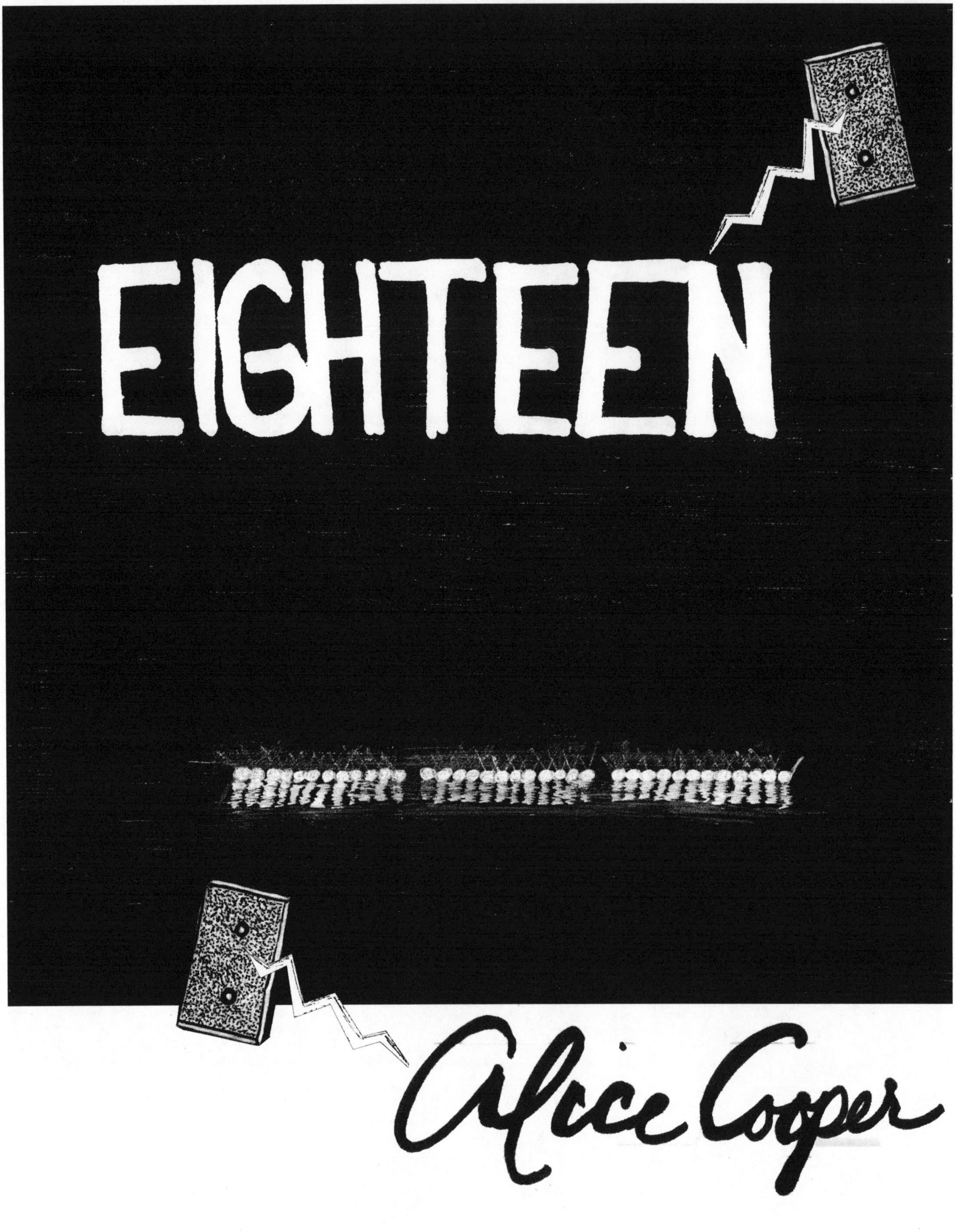
EIGHTEEN
Alice Cooper

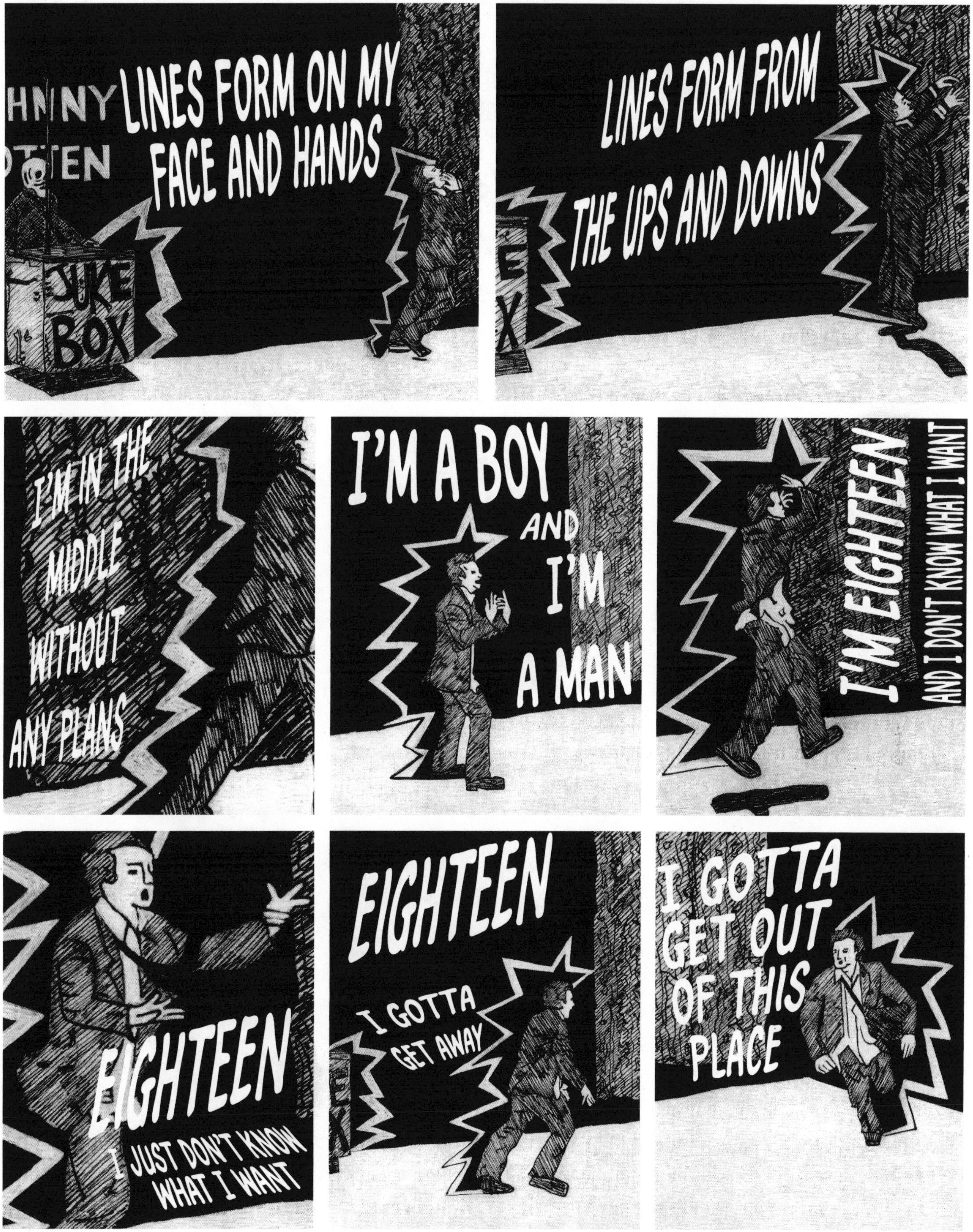

HNNY
TTEN
JUKE BOX
LINES FORM ON MY FACE AND HANDS
LINES FORM FROM THE UPS AND DOWNS
I'M IN THE MIDDLE WITHOUT ANY PLANS
I'M A BOY
AND I'M A MAN
I'M EIGHTEEN
AND I DON'T KNOW WHAT I WANT
EIGHTEEN
I JUST DON'T KNOW WHAT I WANT
EIGHTEEN
I GOTTA GET AWAY
I GOTTA GET OUT OF THIS PLACE

I'LL GO RUNNIN
IN OUTERSPACE
JOHNNY ROTTEN
JUKE BOX
OH YEAH
JOHNNY ROTTEN
JUKE BOX
I GOT A
JOHNNY ROTTEN
BABY'S BRAIN AND AN OLD MAN'S HEART
TOOK EIGHTEEN YEARS TO GET THIS FAR
DON'T ALWAYS KNOW WHAT I'M TALKIN' ABOUT
FEELS LIKE I'M LIVIN' IN THE MIDDLE OF DOUBT
'CAUSE I'M EIGHTEEN
I GET CONFUSED EVERY DAY
EIGHTEEN
I JUST DON'T KNOW WHAT TO SAY
JOHNNY ROTTEN

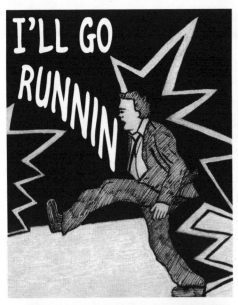

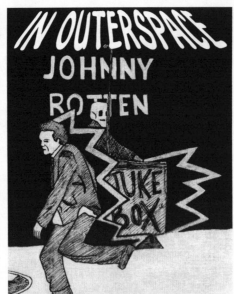

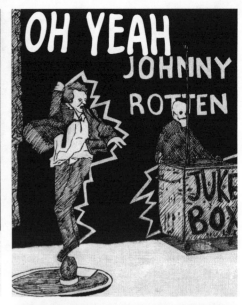

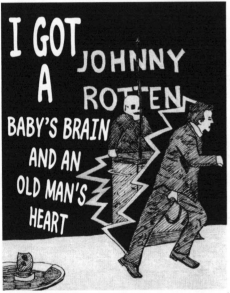

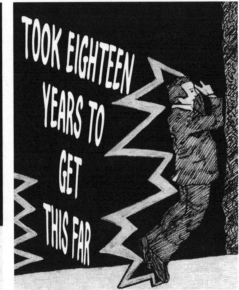

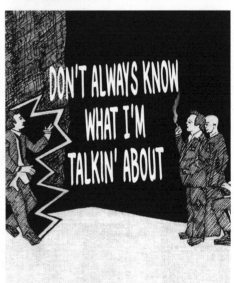

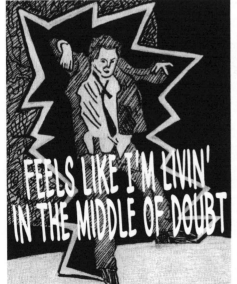

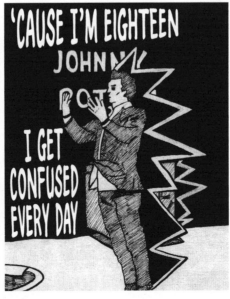

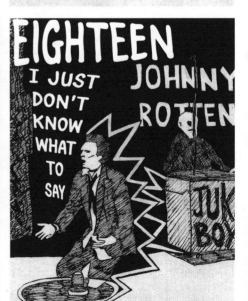

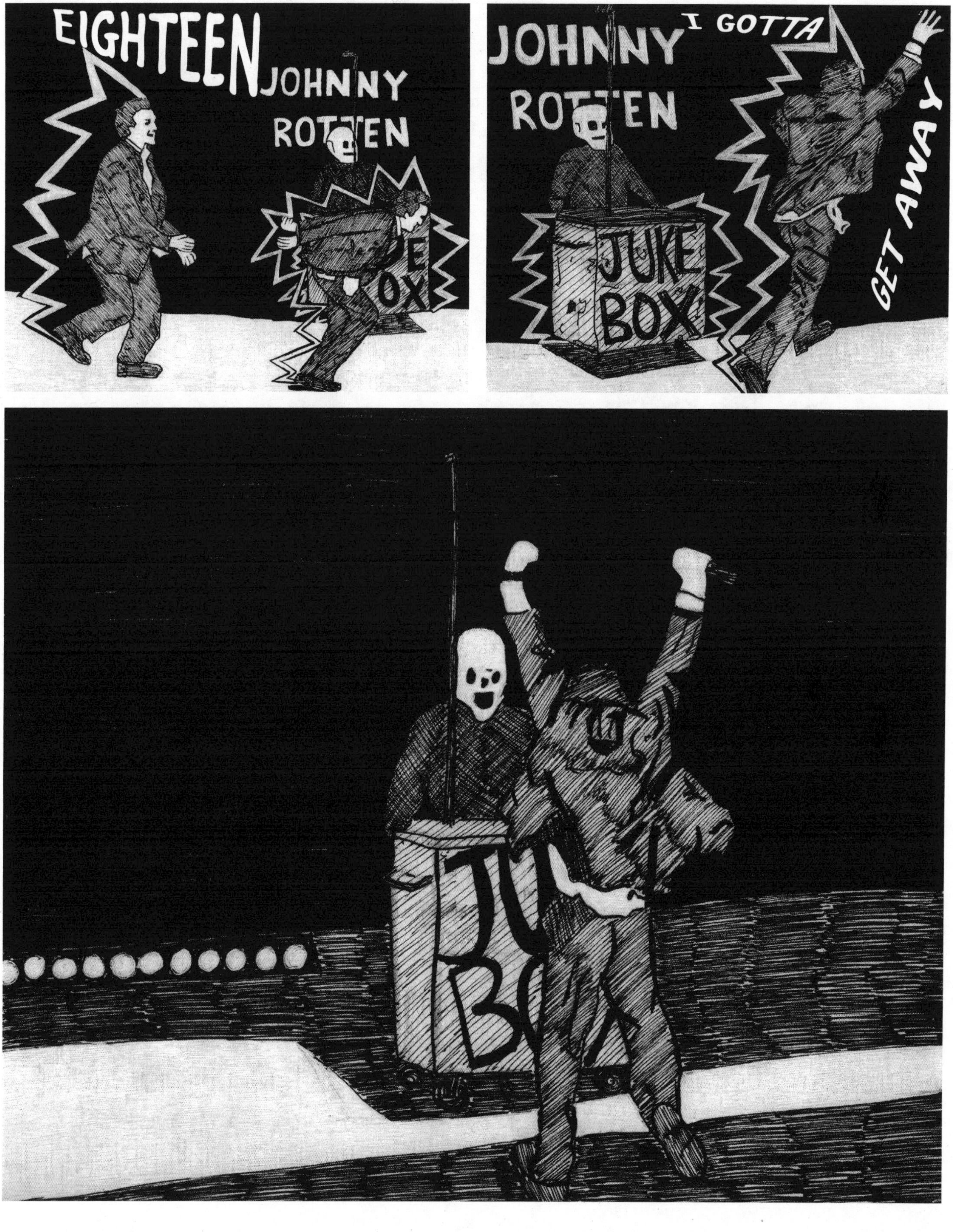
EIGHTEEN
JOHNNY ROTTEN
JOHNNY ROTTEN
JUKE BOX
I GOTTA
GET AWAY

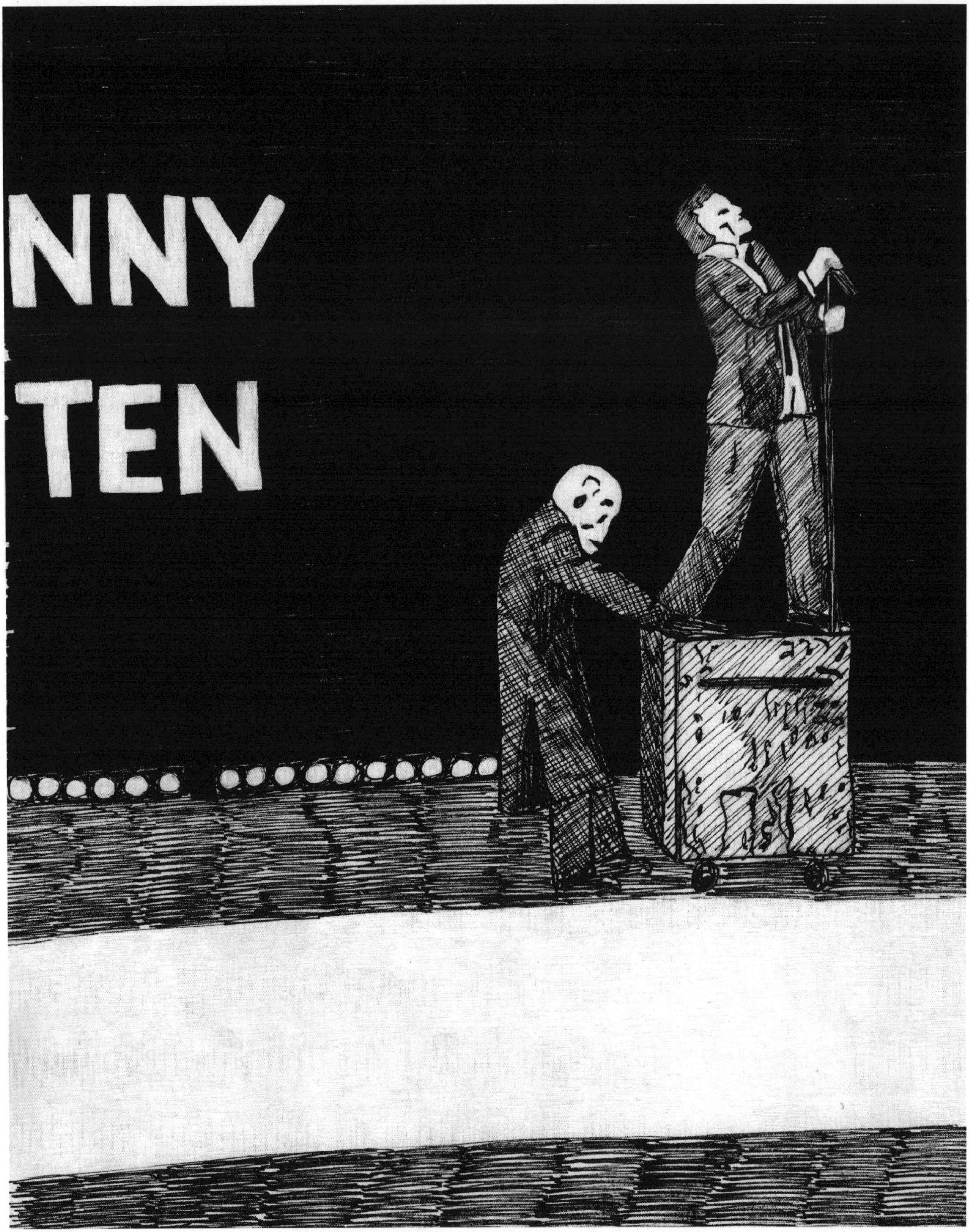
NNY
TEN

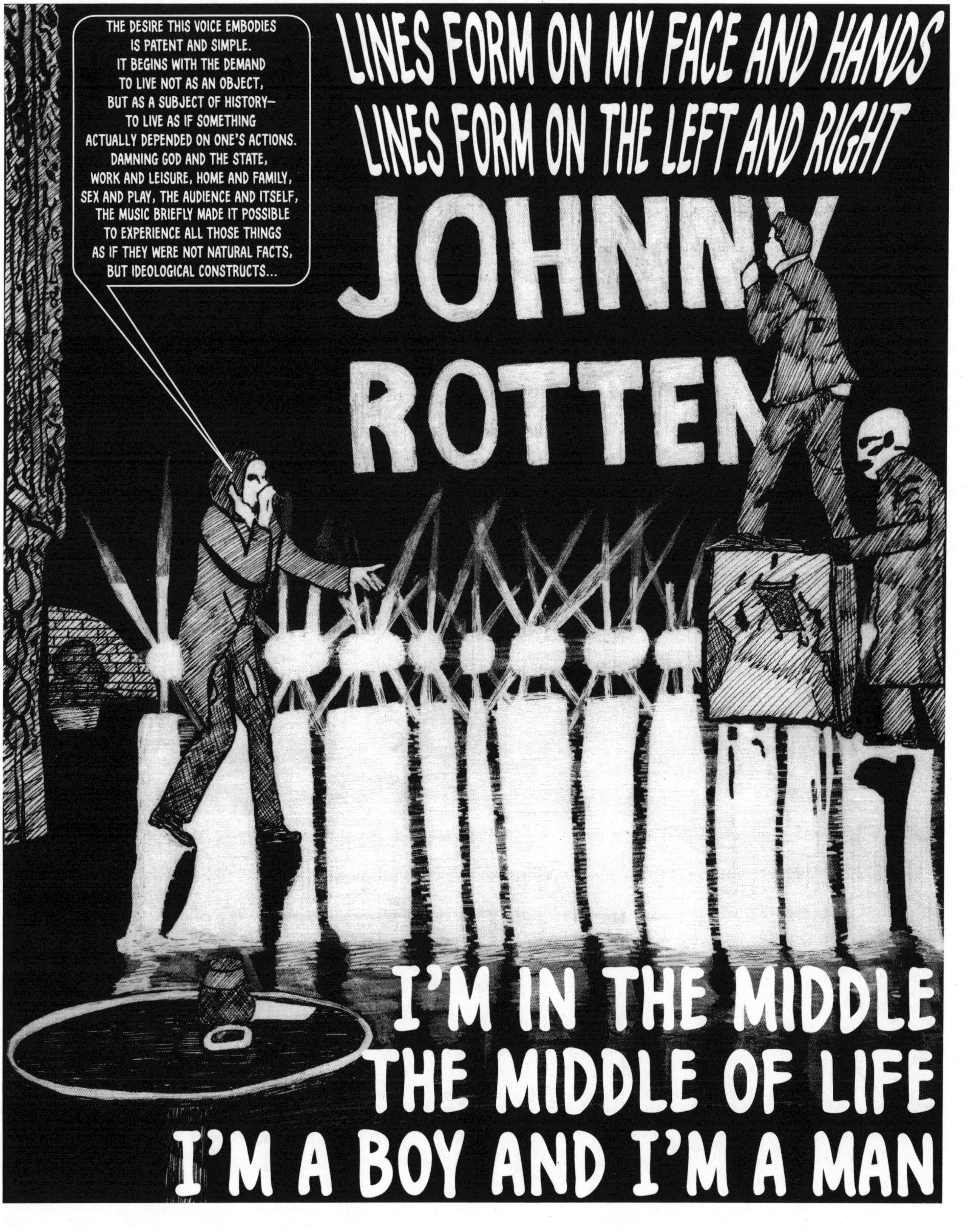
THE DESIRE THIS VOICE EMBODIES IS PATENT AND SIMPLE. IT BEGINS WITH THE DEMAND TO LIVE NOT AS AN OBJECT, BUT AS A SUBJECT OF HISTORY— TO LIVE AS IF SOMETHING ACTUALLY DEPENDED ON ONE'S ACTIONS. DAMNING GOD AND THE STATE, WORK AND LEISURE, HOME AND FAMILY, SEX AND PLAY, THE AUDIENCE AND ITSELF, THE MUSIC BRIEFLY MADE IT POSSIBLE TO EXPERIENCE ALL THOSE THINGS AS IF THEY WERE NOT NATURAL FACTS, BUT IDEOLOGICAL CONSTRUCTS...
LINES FORM ON MY FACE AND HANDS
LINES FORM ON THE LEFT AND RIGHT
JOHNNY
ROTTEN
I'M IN THE MIDDLE
THE MIDDLE OF LIFE
I'M A BOY AND I'M A MAN

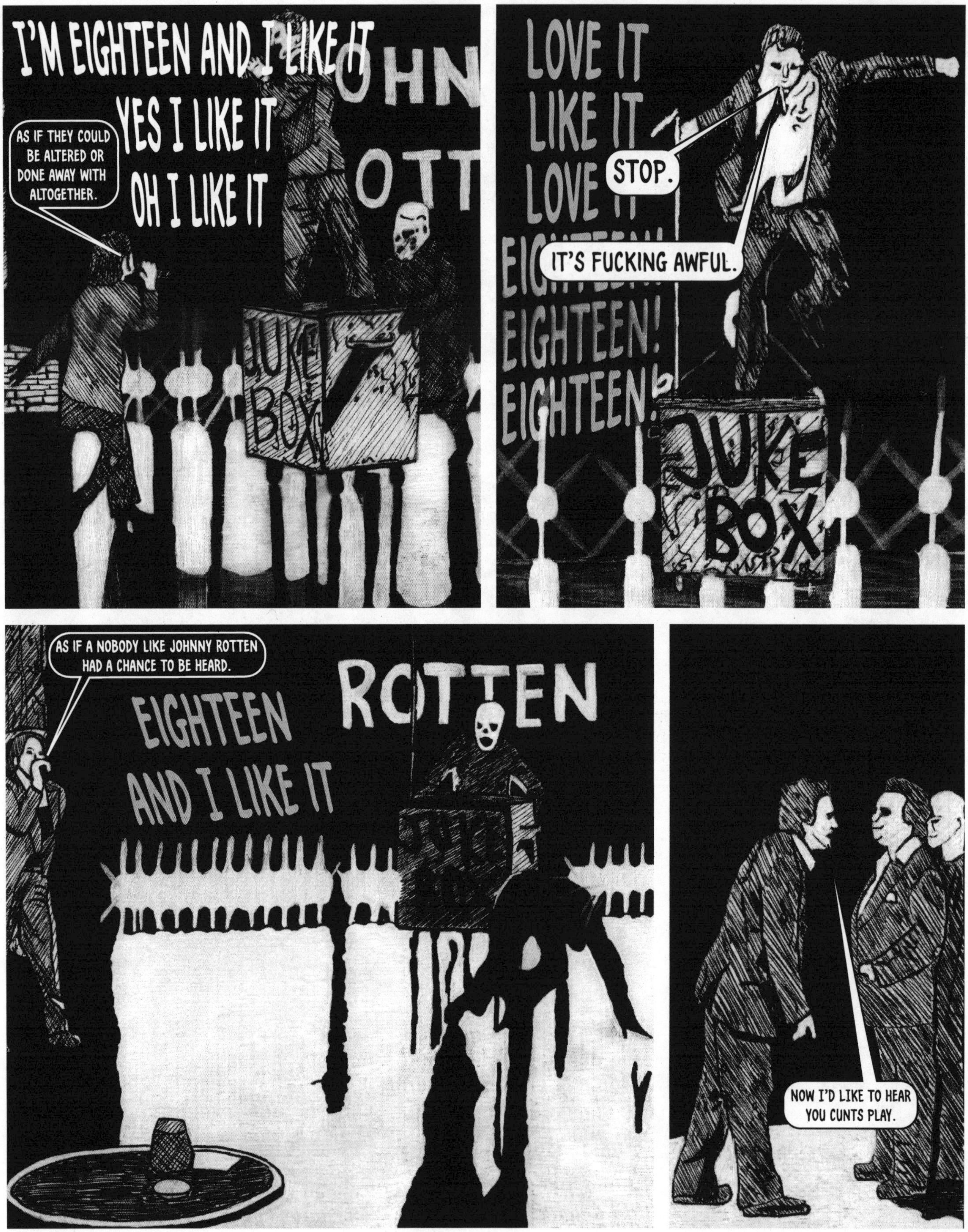
I'M EIGHTEEN AND I LIKE IT
YES I LIKE IT
OH I LIKE IT
AS IF THEY COULD BE ALTERED OR DONE AWAY WITH ALTOGETHER.
JUKE BOX
LOVE IT
LIKE IT
STOP.
IT'S FUCKING AWFUL.
EIGHTEEN!
EIGHTEEN!
JUKE BOX
AS IF A NOBODY LIKE JOHNNY ROTTEN HAD A CHANCE TO BE HEARD.
ROTTEN
EIGHTEEN
AND I LIKE IT
NOW I'D LIKE TO HEAR YOU CUNTS PLAY.

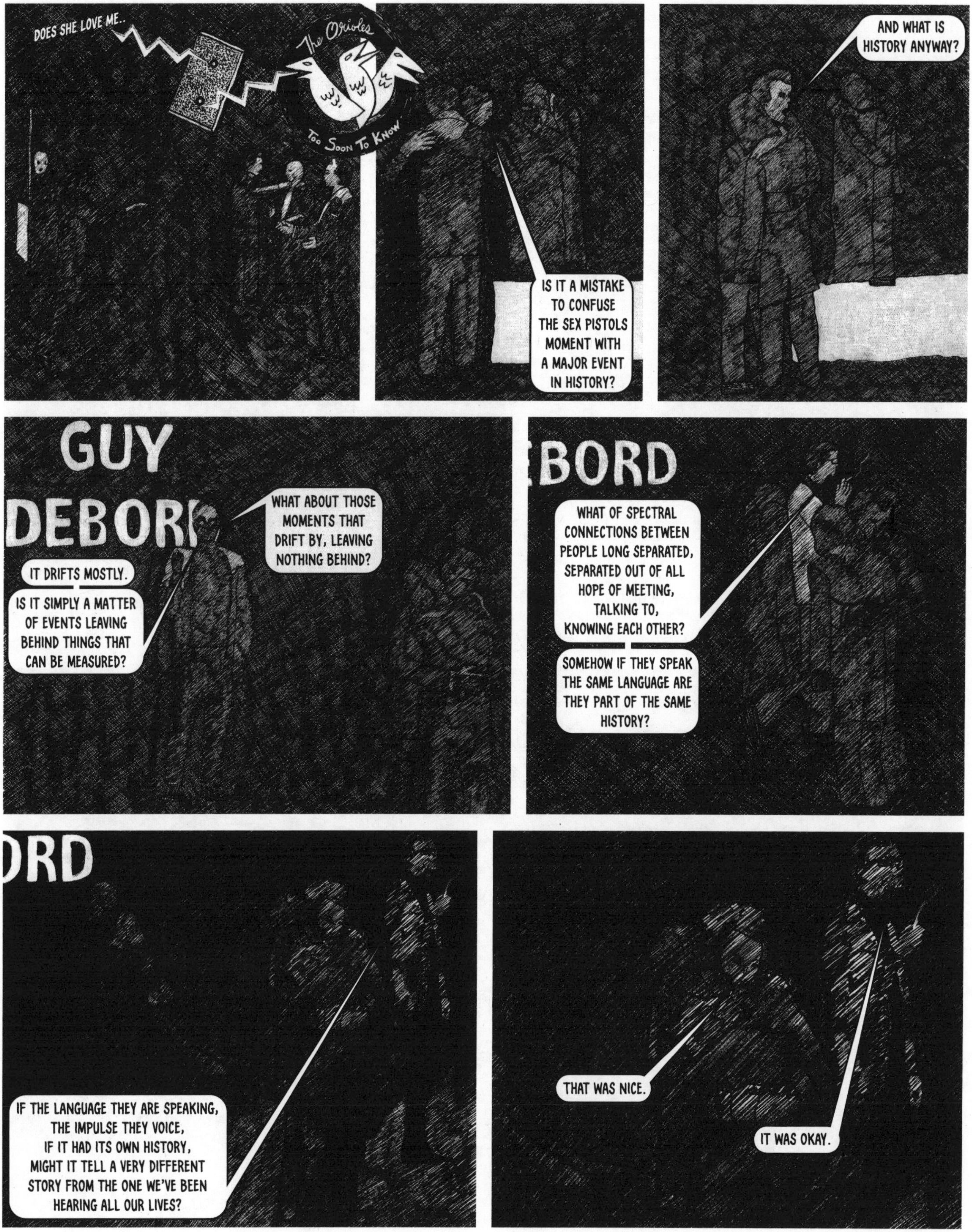
DOES SHE LOVE ME..
The Orioles
Too Soon To Know
IS IT A MISTAKE TO CONFUSE THE SEX PISTOLS MOMENT WITH A MAJOR EVENT IN HISTORY?
AND WHAT IS HISTORY ANYWAY?
GUY DEBORD
WHAT ABOUT THOSE MOMENTS THAT DRIFT BY, LEAVING NOTHING BEHIND?
IT DRIFTS MOSTLY.
IS IT SIMPLY A MATTER OF EVENTS LEAVING BEHIND THINGS THAT CAN BE MEASURED?
EBORD
WHAT OF SPECTRAL CONNECTIONS BETWEEN PEOPLE LONG SEPARATED, SEPARATED OUT OF ALL HOPE OF MEETING, TALKING TO, KNOWING EACH OTHER?
SOMEHOW IF THEY SPEAK THE SAME LANGUAGE ARE THEY PART OF THE SAME HISTORY?
ORD
IF THE LANGUAGE THEY ARE SPEAKING, THE IMPULSE THEY VOICE, IF IT HAD ITS OWN HISTORY, MIGHT IT TELL A VERY DIFFERENT STORY FROM THE ONE WE'VE BEEN HEARING ALL OUR LIVES?
THAT WAS NICE.
IT WAS OKAY.

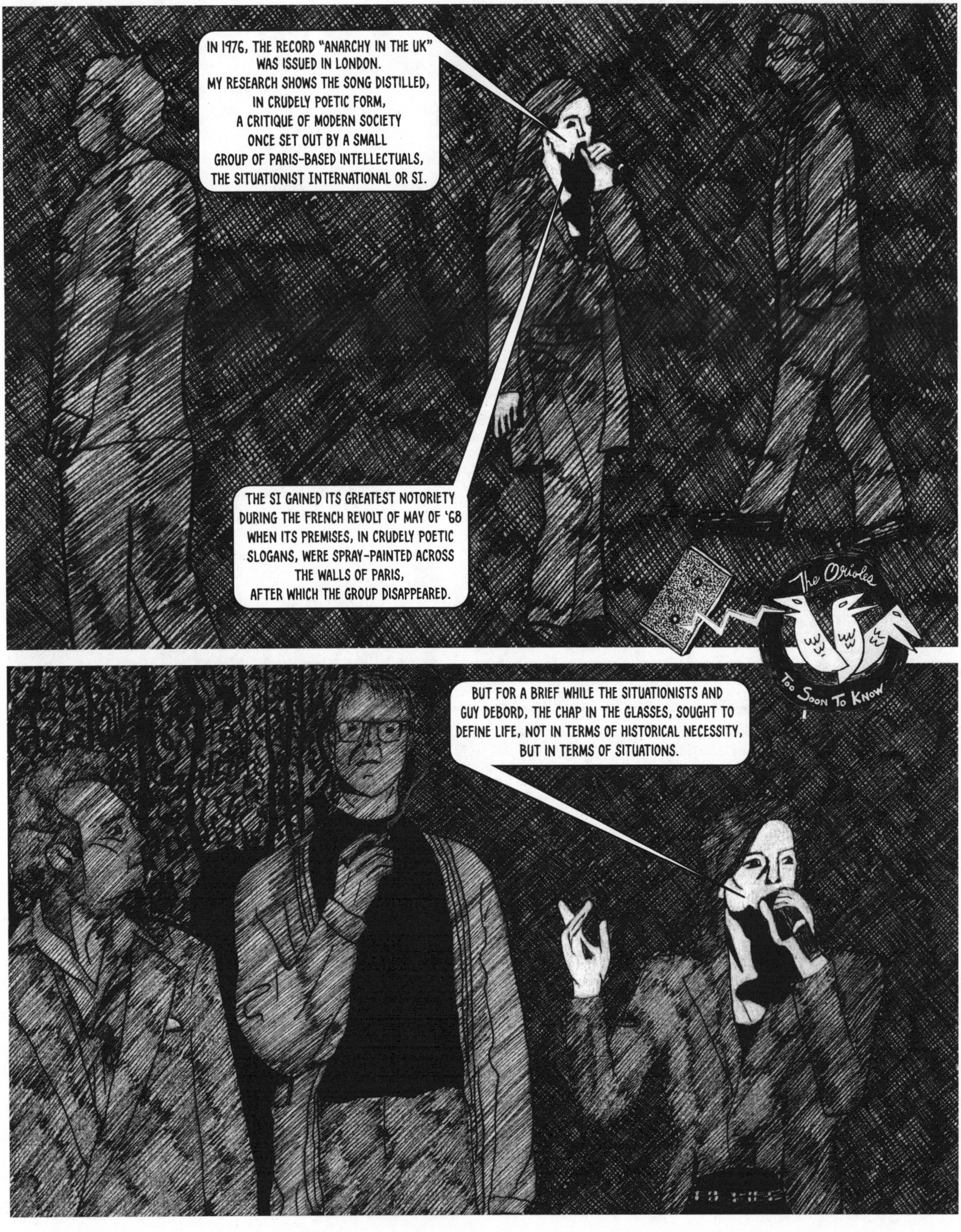
IN 1976, THE RECORD "ANARCHY IN THE UK" WAS ISSUED IN LONDON. MY RESEARCH SHOWS THE SONG DISTILLED, IN CRUDELY POETIC FORM, A CRITIQUE OF MODERN SOCIETY ONCE SET OUT BY A SMALL GROUP OF PARIS-BASED INTELLECTUALS, THE SITUATIONIST INTERNATIONAL OR SI.
THE SI GAINED ITS GREATEST NOTORIETY DURING THE FRENCH REVOLT OF MAY OF '68 WHEN ITS PREMISES, IN CRUDELY POETIC SLOGANS, WERE SPRAY-PAINTED ACROSS THE WALLS OF PARIS, AFTER WHICH THE GROUP DISAPPEARED.
The Orioles
Too Soon To Know
BUT FOR A BRIEF WHILE THE SITUATIONISTS AND GUY DEBORD, THE CHAP IN THE GLASSES, SOUGHT TO DEFINE LIFE, NOT IN TERMS OF HISTORICAL NECESSITY, BUT IN TERMS OF SITUATIONS.

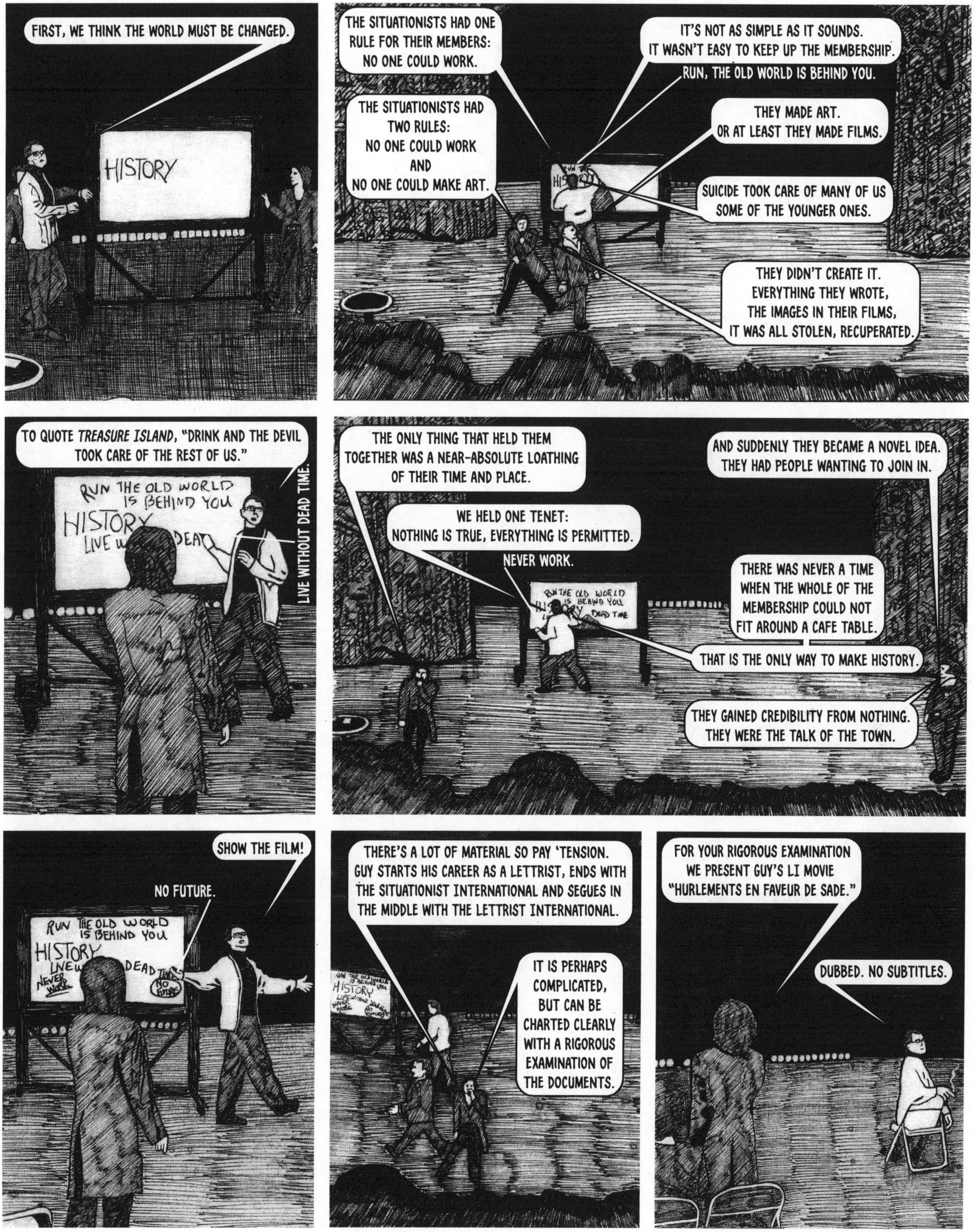
FIRST, WE THINK THE WORLD MUST BE CHANGED.
HISTORY
THE SITUATIONISTS HAD ONE RULE FOR THEIR MEMBERS: NO ONE COULD WORK.
IT'S NOT AS SIMPLE AS IT SOUNDS. IT WASN'T EASY TO KEEP UP THE MEMBERSHIP.
RUN, THE OLD WORLD IS BEHIND YOU.
THE SITUATIONISTS HAD TWO RULES: NO ONE COULD WORK AND NO ONE COULD MAKE ART.
THEY MADE ART. OR AT LEAST THEY MADE FILMS.
SUICIDE TOOK CARE OF MANY OF US SOME OF THE YOUNGER ONES.
THEY DIDN'T CREATE IT. EVERYTHING THEY WROTE, THE IMAGES IN THEIR FILMS, IT WAS ALL STOLEN, RECUPERATED.
TO QUOTE *TREASURE ISLAND*, "DRINK AND THE DEVIL TOOK CARE OF THE REST OF US."
RUN THE OLD WORLD IS BEHIND YOU
HISTORY
LIVE WITHOUT DEAD TIME.
THE ONLY THING THAT HELD THEM TOGETHER WAS A NEAR-ABSOLUTE LOATHING OF THEIR TIME AND PLACE.
WE HELD ONE TENET: NOTHING IS TRUE, EVERYTHING IS PERMITTED.
NEVER WORK.
AND SUDDENLY THEY BECAME A NOVEL IDEA. THEY HAD PEOPLE WANTING TO JOIN IN.
THERE WAS NEVER A TIME WHEN THE WHOLE OF THE MEMBERSHIP COULD NOT FIT AROUND A CAFE TABLE.
THAT IS THE ONLY WAY TO MAKE HISTORY.
THEY GAINED CREDIBILITY FROM NOTHING. THEY WERE THE TALK OF THE TOWN.
SHOW THE FILM!
NO FUTURE.
RUN THE OLD WORLD IS BEHIND YOU
HISTORY
NEVER WORK
NO FUTURE
THERE'S A LOT OF MATERIAL SO PAY 'TENSION. GUY STARTS HIS CAREER AS A LETTRIST, ENDS WITH THE SITUATIONIST INTERNATIONAL AND SEGUES IN THE MIDDLE WITH THE LETTRIST INTERNATIONAL.
IT IS PERHAPS COMPLICATED, BUT CAN BE CHARTED CLEARLY WITH A RIGOROUS EXAMINATION OF THE DOCUMENTS.
FOR YOUR RIGOROUS EXAMINATION WE PRESENT GUY'S LI MOVIE "HURLEMENTS EN FAVEUR DE SADE."
DUBBED. NO SUBTITLES.

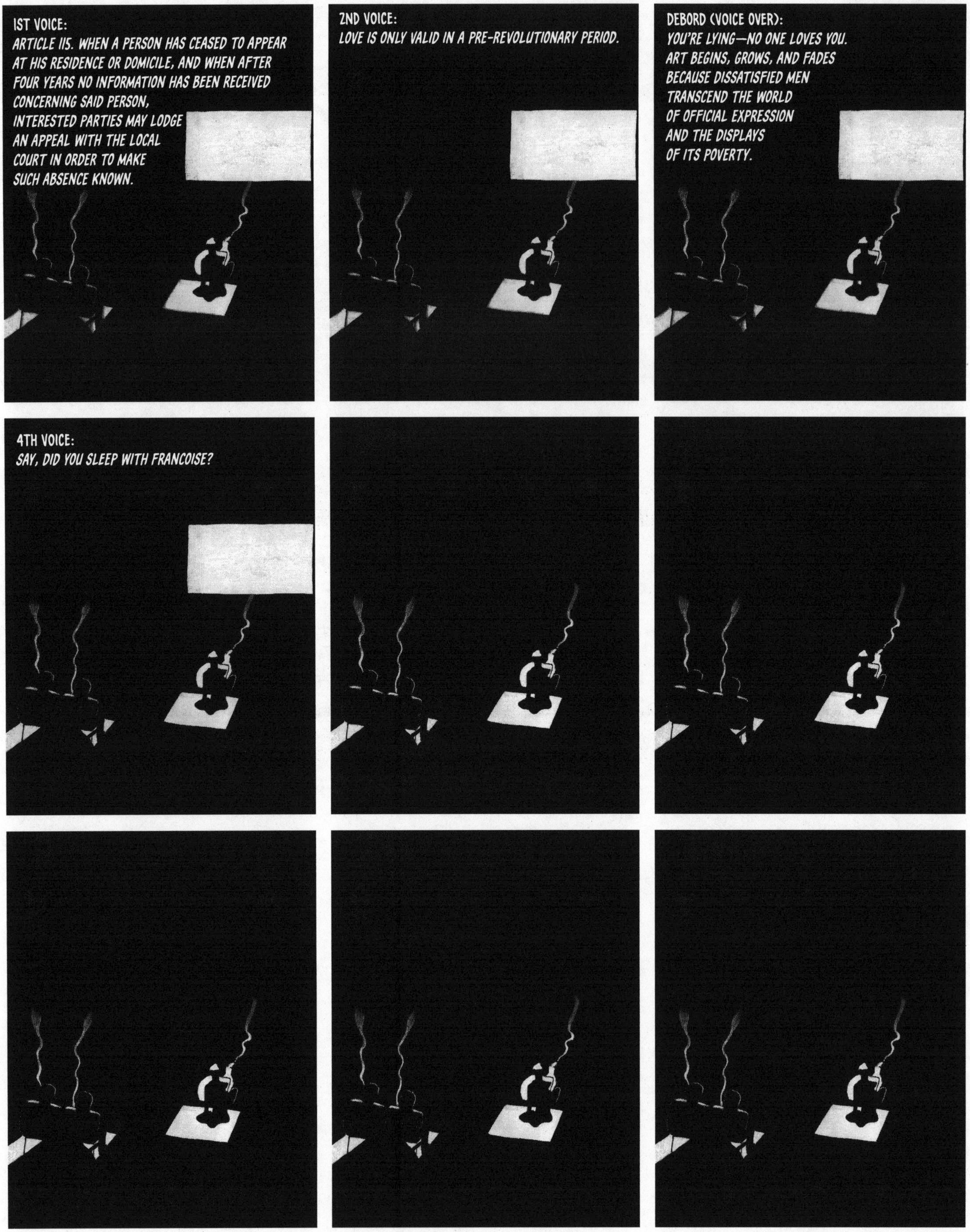
1ST VOICE:
ARTICLE 115. WHEN A PERSON HAS CEASED TO APPEAR AT HIS RESIDENCE OR DOMICILE, AND WHEN AFTER FOUR YEARS NO INFORMATION HAS BEEN RECEIVED CONCERNING SAID PERSON, INTERESTED PARTIES MAY LODGE AN APPEAL WITH THE LOCAL COURT IN ORDER TO MAKE SUCH ABSENCE KNOWN.
2ND VOICE:
LOVE IS ONLY VALID IN A PRE-REVOLUTIONARY PERIOD.
DEBORD (VOICE OVER):
YOU'RE LYING—NO ONE LOVES YOU. ART BEGINS, GROWS, AND FADES BECAUSE DISSATISFIED MEN TRANSCEND THE WORLD OF OFFICIAL EXPRESSION AND THE DISPLAYS OF ITS POVERTY.
4TH VOICE:
SAY, DID YOU SLEEP WITH FRANCOISE?

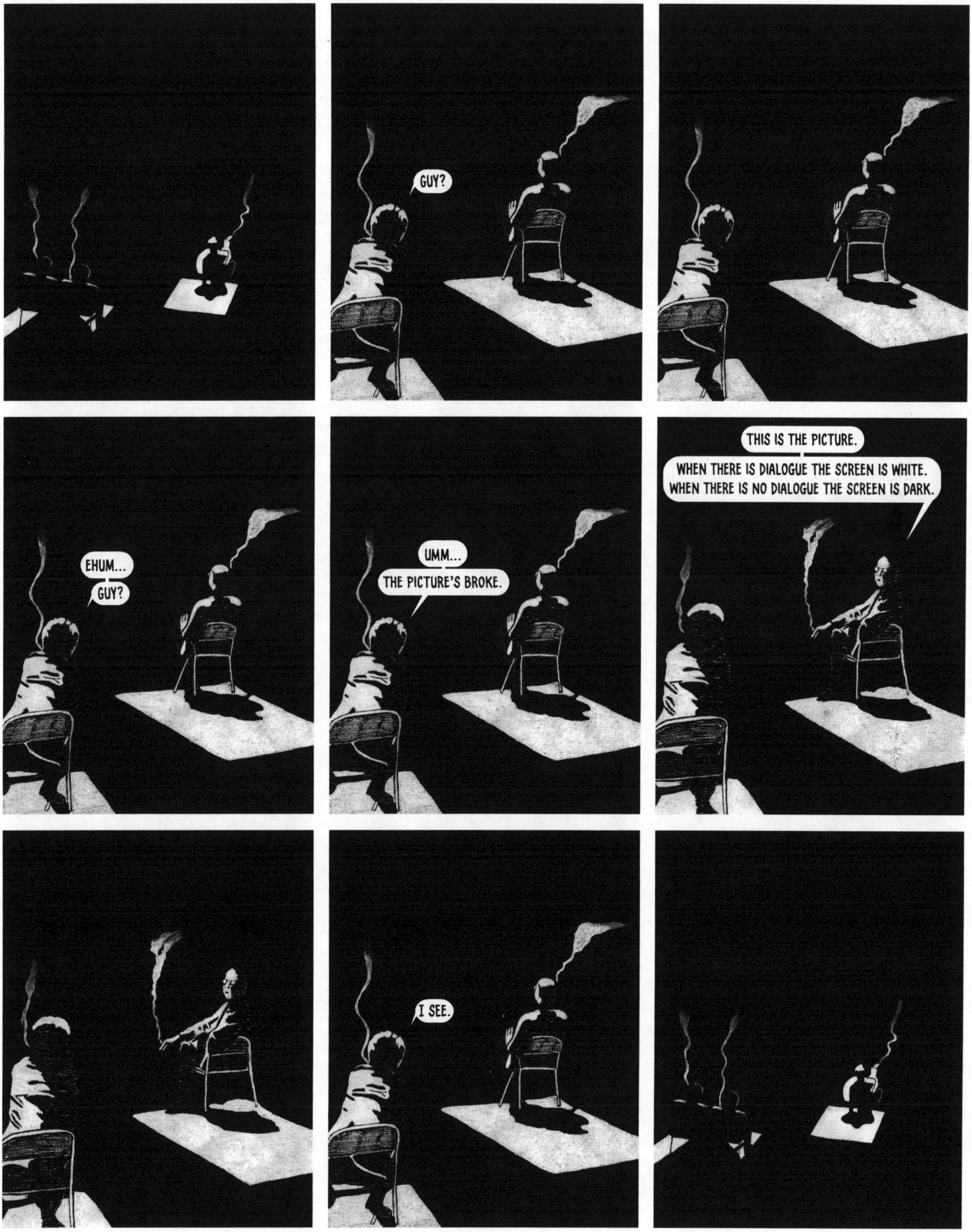
GUY?
EHUM...
GUY?
UMM...
THE PICTURE'S BROKE.
THIS IS THE PICTURE.
WHEN THERE IS DIALOGUE THE SCREEN IS WHITE.
WHEN THERE IS NO DIALOGUE THE SCREEN IS DARK.
I SEE.

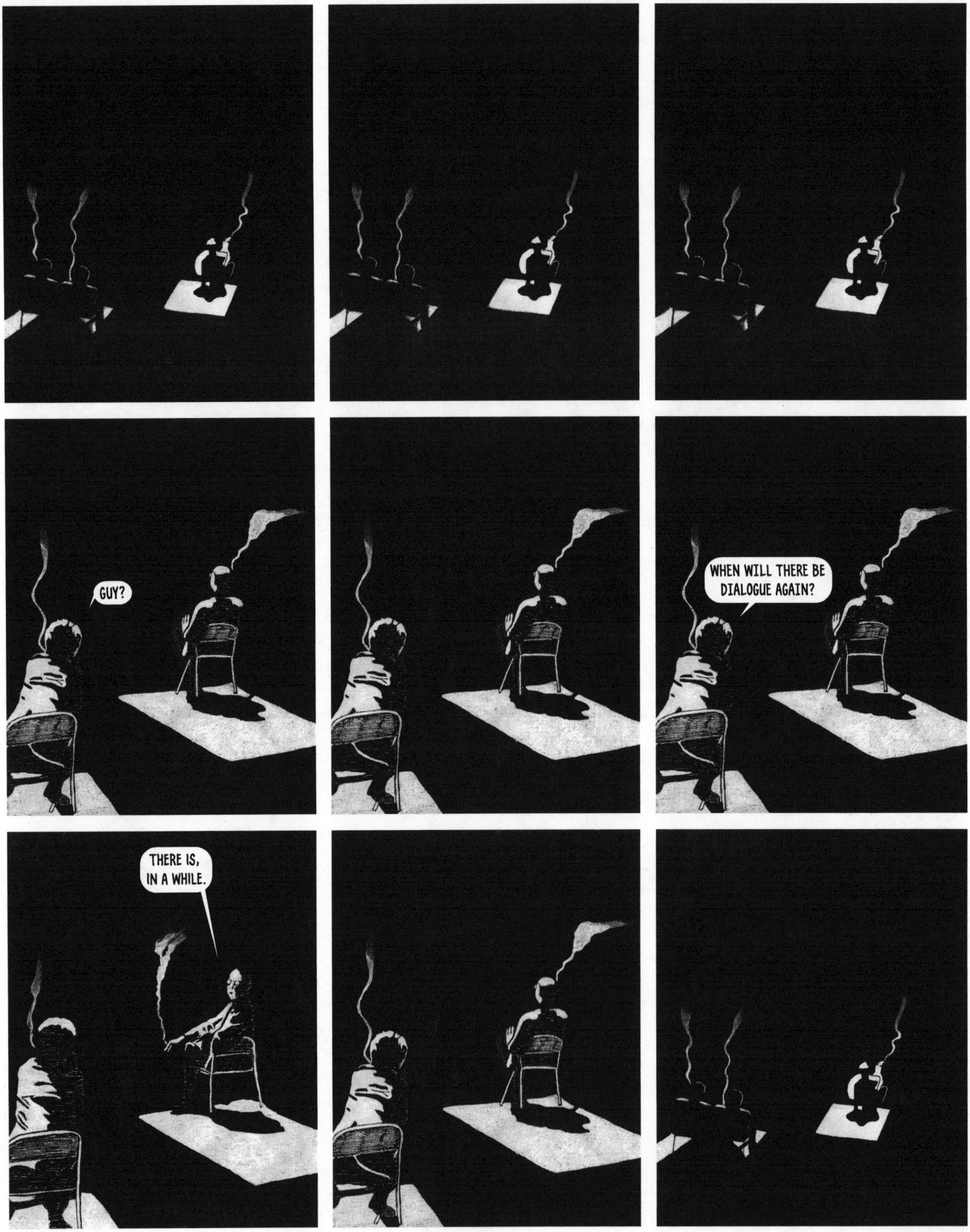
GUY?
WHEN WILL THERE BE DIALOGUE AGAIN?
THERE IS, IN A WHILE.

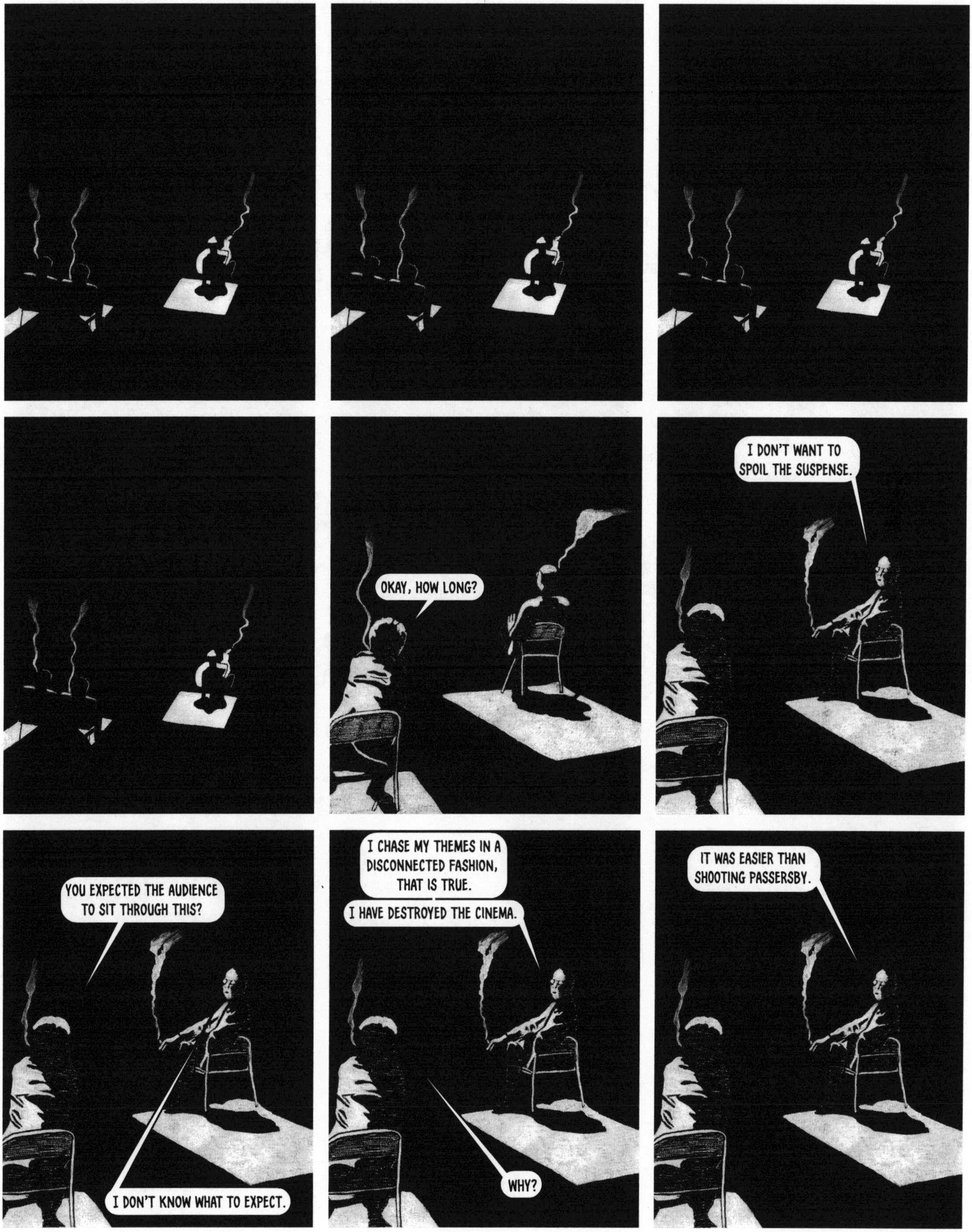
OKAY, HOW LONG?
I DON'T WANT TO SPOIL THE SUSPENSE.
YOU EXPECTED THE AUDIENCE TO SIT THROUGH THIS?
I DON'T KNOW WHAT TO EXPECT.
I CHASE MY THEMES IN A DISCONNECTED FASHION, THAT IS TRUE.
I HAVE DESTROYED THE CINEMA.
WHY?
IT WAS EASIER THAN SHOOTING PASSERSBY.

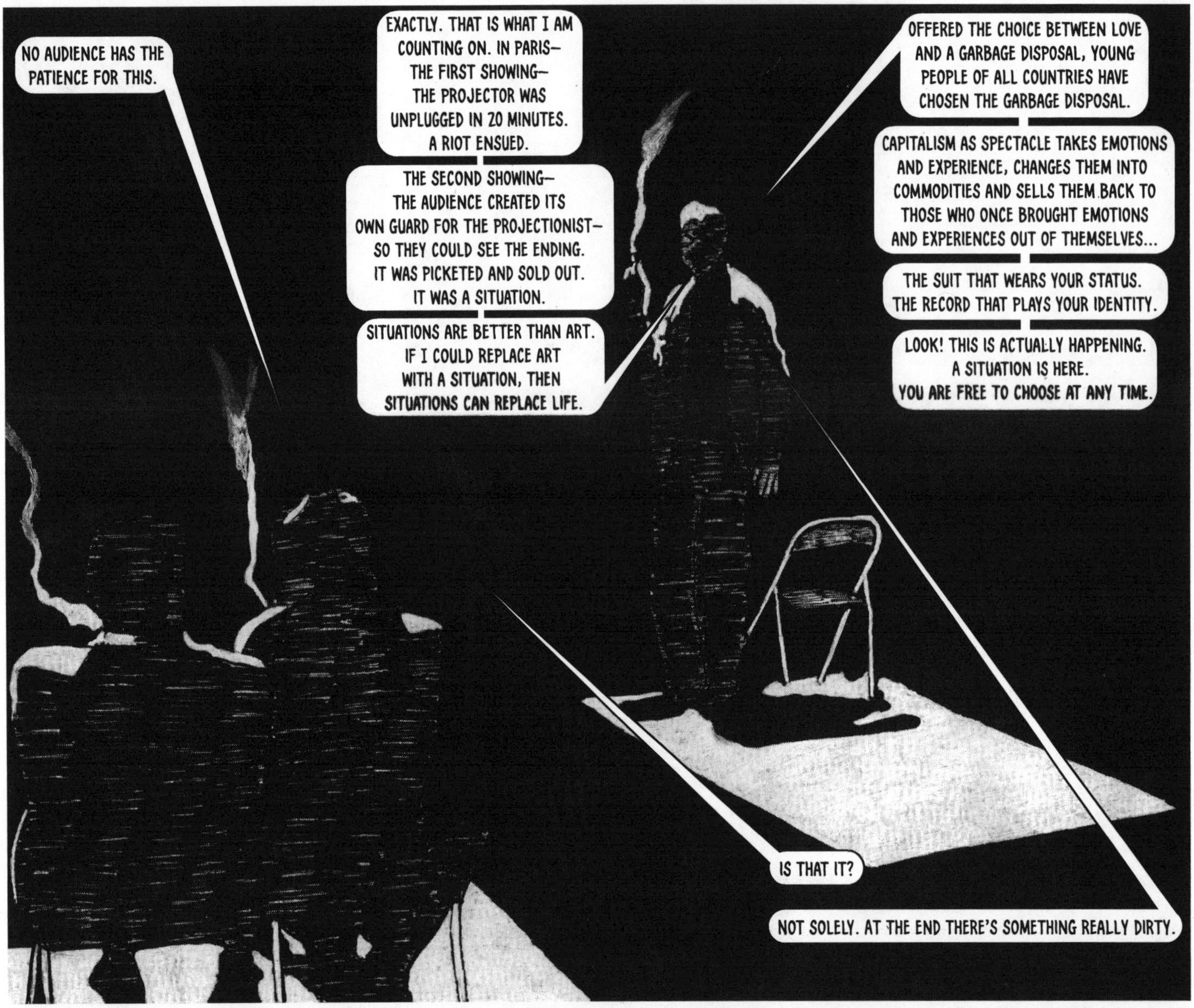
NO AUDIENCE HAS THE PATIENCE FOR THIS.
EXACTLY. THAT IS WHAT I AM COUNTING ON. IN PARIS— THE FIRST SHOWING— THE PROJECTOR WAS UNPLUGGED IN 20 MINUTES. A RIOT ENSUED.
THE SECOND SHOWING— THE AUDIENCE CREATED ITS OWN GUARD FOR THE PROJECTIONIST— SO THEY COULD SEE THE ENDING. IT WAS PICKETED AND SOLD OUT. IT WAS A SITUATION.
SITUATIONS ARE BETTER THAN ART. IF I COULD REPLACE ART WITH A SITUATION, THEN SITUATIONS CAN REPLACE LIFE.
OFFERED THE CHOICE BETWEEN LOVE AND A GARBAGE DISPOSAL, YOUNG PEOPLE OF ALL COUNTRIES HAVE CHOSEN THE GARBAGE DISPOSAL.
CAPITALISM AS SPECTACLE TAKES EMOTIONS AND EXPERIENCE, CHANGES THEM INTO COMMODITIES AND SELLS THEM BACK TO THOSE WHO ONCE BROUGHT EMOTIONS AND EXPERIENCES OUT OF THEMSELVES...
THE SUIT THAT WEARS YOUR STATUS. THE RECORD THAT PLAYS YOUR IDENTITY.
LOOK! THIS IS ACTUALLY HAPPENING. A SITUATION IS HERE. YOU ARE FREE TO CHOOSE AT ANY TIME.
IS THAT IT?
NOT SOLELY. AT THE END THERE'S SOMETHING REALLY DIRTY.

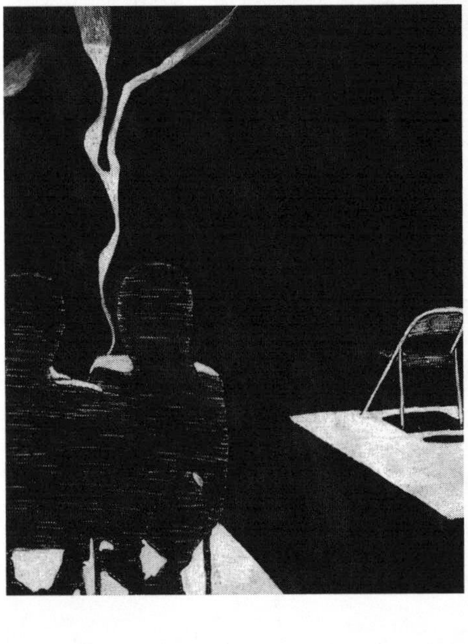

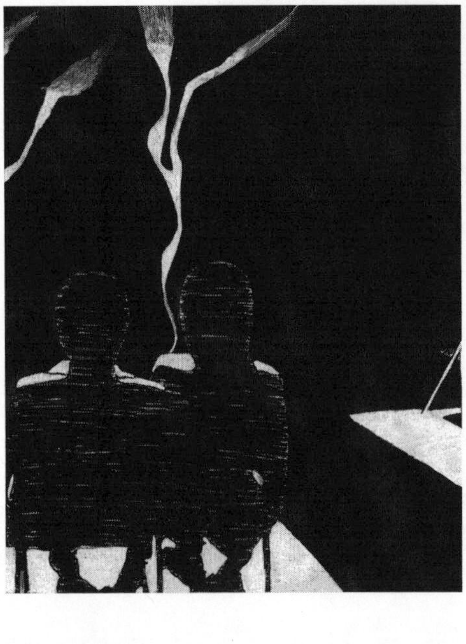

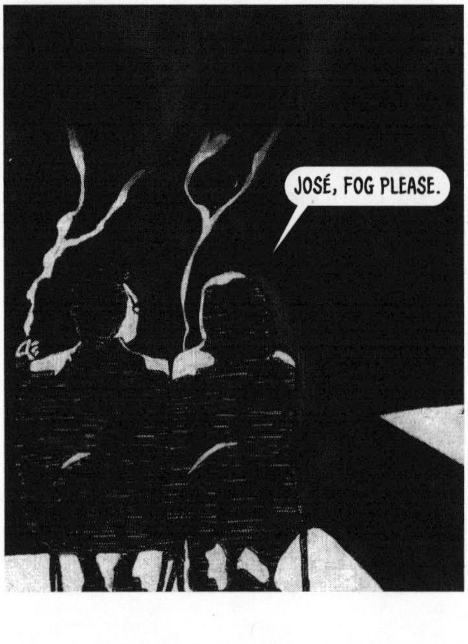
JOSÉ, FOG PLEASE.

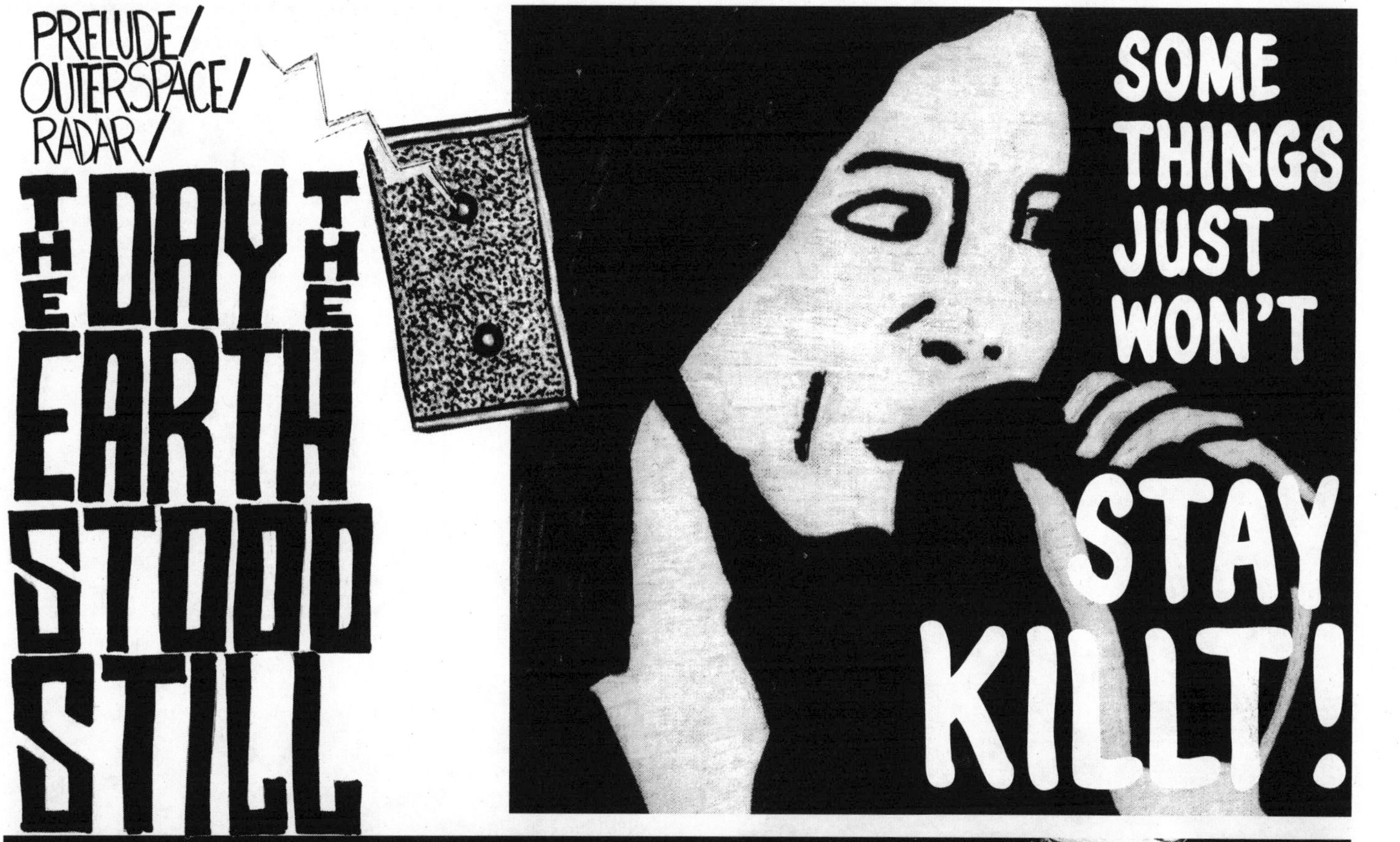
PRELUDE/
OUTERSPACE/
RADAR/
THE DAY THE EARTH STOOD STILL
SOME THINGS JUST WON'T
STAY KILLT!

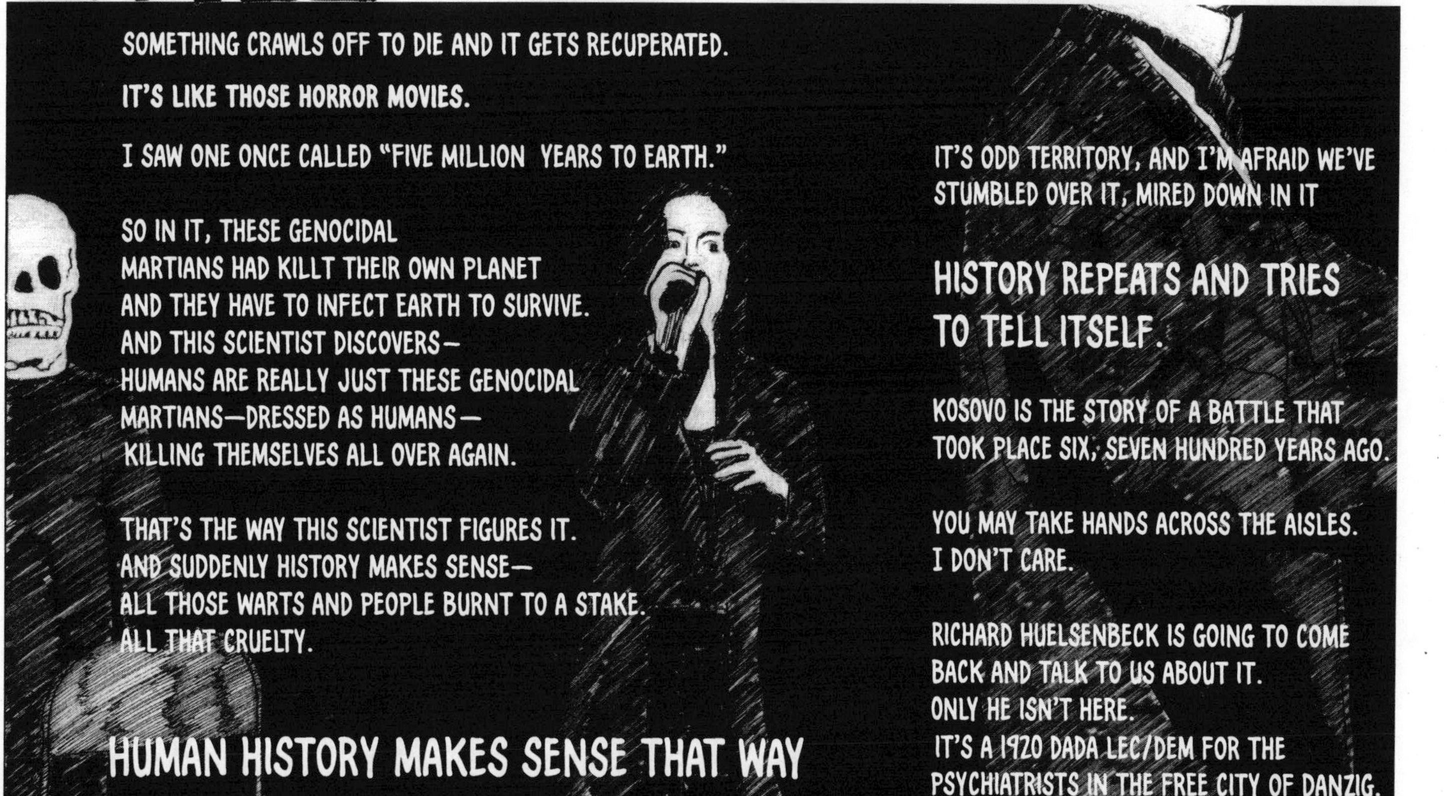
SOMETHING CRAWLS OFF TO DIE AND IT GETS RECUPERATED.
IT'S LIKE THOSE HORROR MOVIES.
I SAW ONE ONCE CALLED "FIVE MILLION YEARS TO EARTH."
SO IN IT, THESE GENOCIDAL
MARTIANS HAD KILLT THEIR OWN PLANET
AND THEY HAVE TO INFECT EARTH TO SURVIVE.
AND THIS SCIENTIST DISCOVERS—
HUMANS ARE REALLY JUST THESE GENOCIDAL
MARTIANS—DRESSED AS HUMANS—
KILLING THEMSELVES ALL OVER AGAIN.
THAT'S THE WAY THIS SCIENTIST FIGURES IT.
AND SUDDENLY HISTORY MAKES SENSE—
ALL THOSE WARTS AND PEOPLE BURNT TO A STAKE.
ALL THAT CRUELTY.
HUMAN HISTORY MAKES SENSE THAT WAY
. . . BUT IT ISN'T HUMAN!
IT'S ODD TERRITORY, AND I'M AFRAID WE'VE
STUMBLED OVER IT, MIRED DOWN IN IT
HISTORY REPEATS AND TRIES
TO TELL ITSELF.
KOSOVO IS THE STORY OF A BATTLE THAT
TOOK PLACE SIX, SEVEN HUNDRED YEARS AGO.
YOU MAY TAKE HANDS ACROSS THE AISLES.
I DON'T CARE.
RICHARD HUELSENBECK IS GOING TO COME
BACK AND TALK TO US ABOUT IT.
ONLY HE ISN'T HERE.
IT'S A 1920 DADA LEC/DEM FOR THE
PSYCHIATRISTS IN THE FREE CITY OF DANZIG.
UNLESS YOU CALL IT GDANSK.

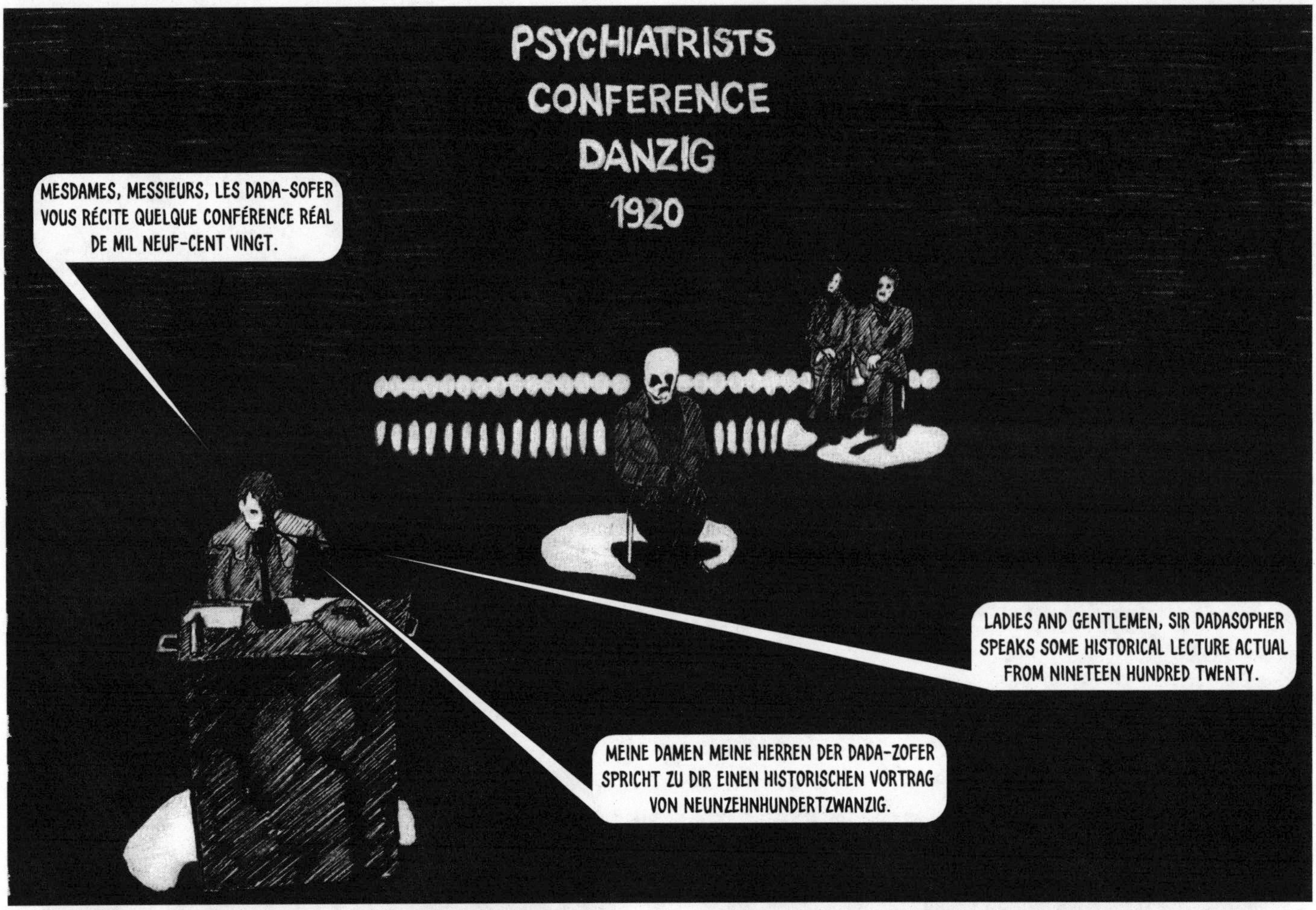
PSYCHIATRISTS
CONFERENCE
DANZIG
1920
MESDAMES, MESSIEURS, LES DADA-SOFER VOUS RÉCITE QUELQUE CONFÉRENCE RÉAL DE MIL NEUF-CENT VINGT.
LADIES AND GENTLEMEN, SIR DADASOPHER SPEAKS SOME HISTORICAL LECTURE ACTUAL FROM NINETEEN HUNDRED TWENTY.
MEINE DAMEN MEINE HERREN DER DADA-ZOFER SPRICHT ZU DIR EINEN HISTORISCHEN VORTRAG VON NEUNZEHNHUNDERTZWANZIG.

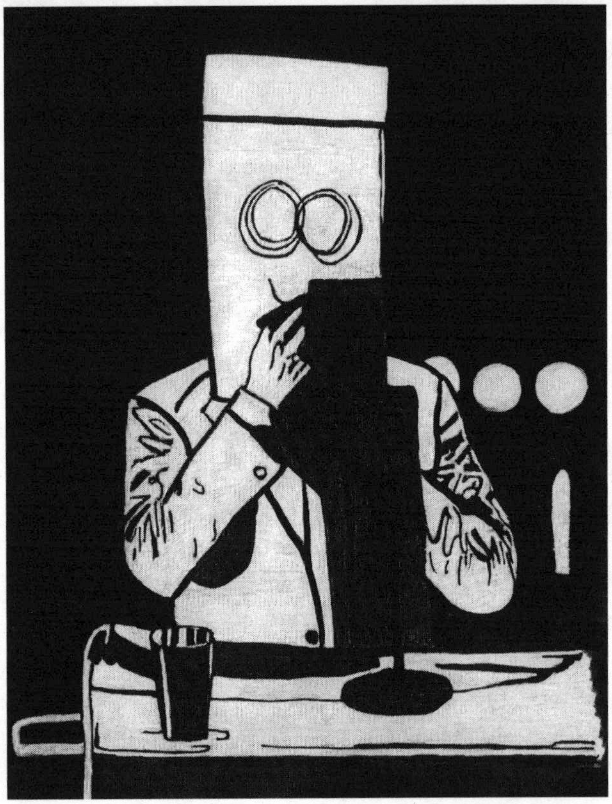

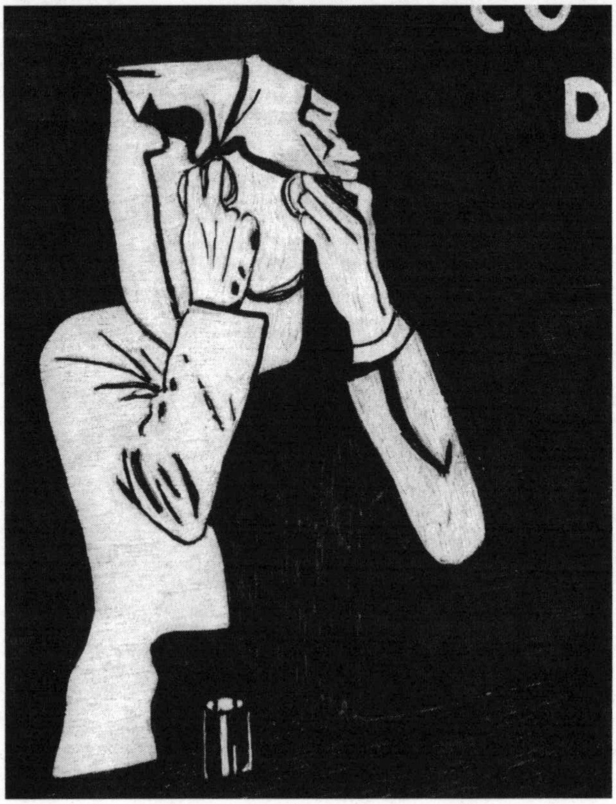

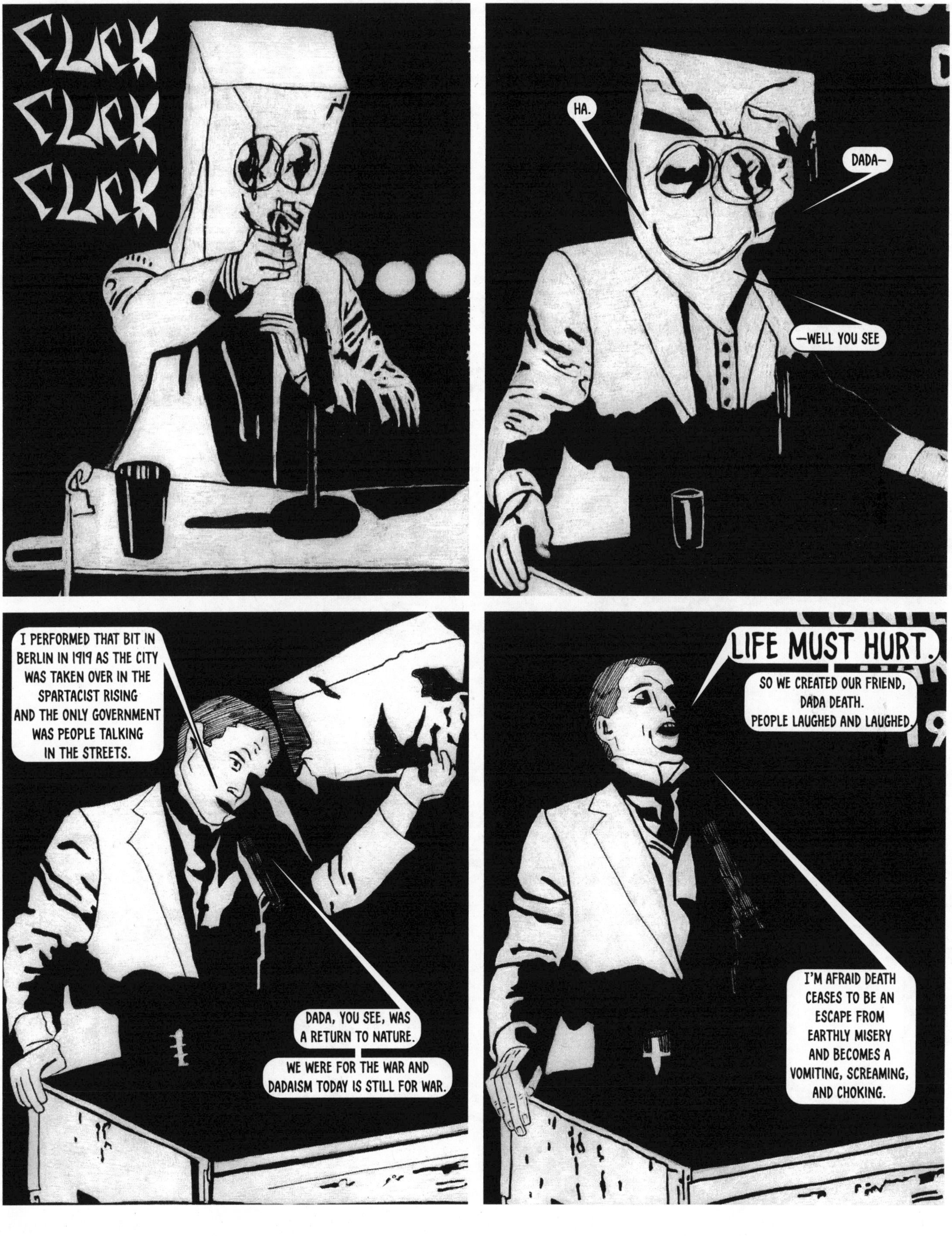
CLICK
CLICK
CLICK
HA.
DADA–
—WELL YOU SEE
I PERFORMED THAT BIT IN BERLIN IN 1919 AS THE CITY WAS TAKEN OVER IN THE SPARTACIST RISING AND THE ONLY GOVERNMENT WAS PEOPLE TALKING IN THE STREETS.
DADA, YOU SEE, WAS A RETURN TO NATURE.
WE WERE FOR THE WAR AND DADAISM TODAY IS STILL FOR WAR.
LIFE MUST HURT.
SO WE CREATED OUR FRIEND, DADA DEATH. PEOPLE LAUGHED AND LAUGHED.
I'M AFRAID DEATH CEASES TO BE AN ESCAPE FROM EARTHLY MISERY AND BECOMES A VOMITING, SCREAMING, AND CHOKING.

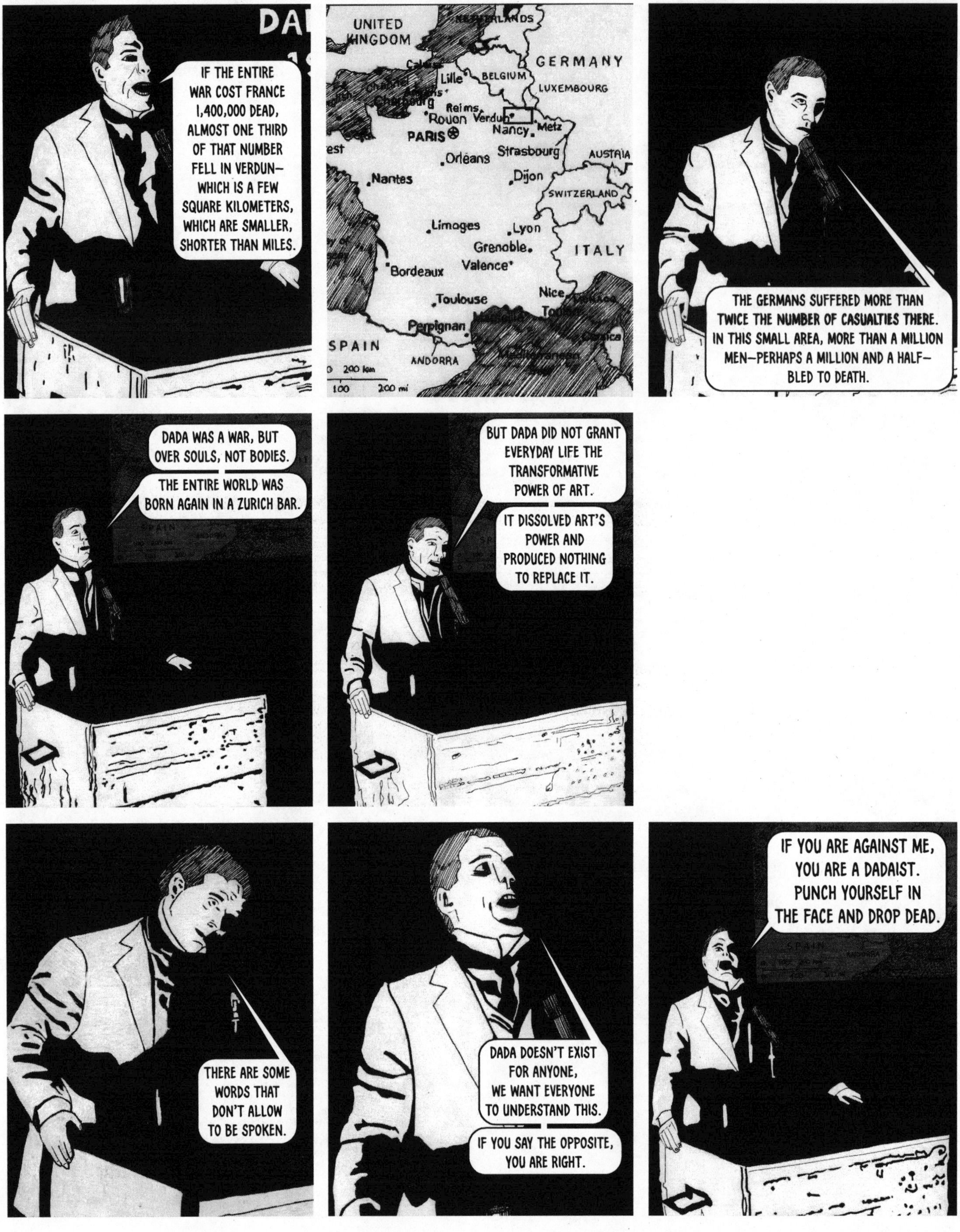
IF THE ENTIRE WAR COST FRANCE 1,400,000 DEAD, ALMOST ONE THIRD OF THAT NUMBER FELL IN VERDUN— WHICH IS A FEW SQUARE KILOMETERS, WHICH ARE SMALLER, SHORTER THAN MILES.
UNITED KINGDOM
GERMANY
BELGIUM
LUXEMBOURG
Lille
Reims
Rouen
Verdun
Metz
Nancy
PARIS
Orléans
Strasbourg
AUSTRIA
Nantes
Dijon
SWITZERLAND
Limoges
Lyon
Grenoble
ITALY
Bordeaux
Valence
Toulouse
Nice
Perpignan
SPAIN
ANDORRA
200 km
100
200 mi
THE GERMANS SUFFERED MORE THAN TWICE THE NUMBER OF CASUALTIES THERE. IN THIS SMALL AREA, MORE THAN A MILLION MEN—PERHAPS A MILLION AND A HALF— BLED TO DEATH.
DADA WAS A WAR, BUT OVER SOULS, NOT BODIES.
THE ENTIRE WORLD WAS BORN AGAIN IN A ZURICH BAR.
BUT DADA DID NOT GRANT EVERYDAY LIFE THE TRANSFORMATIVE POWER OF ART.
IT DISSOLVED ART'S POWER AND PRODUCED NOTHING TO REPLACE IT.
THERE ARE SOME WORDS THAT DON'T ALLOW TO BE SPOKEN.
DADA DOESN'T EXIST FOR ANYONE, WE WANT EVERYONE TO UNDERSTAND THIS.
IF YOU SAY THE OPPOSITE, YOU ARE RIGHT.
IF YOU ARE AGAINST ME, YOU ARE A DADAIST. PUNCH YOURSELF IN THE FACE AND DROP DEAD.

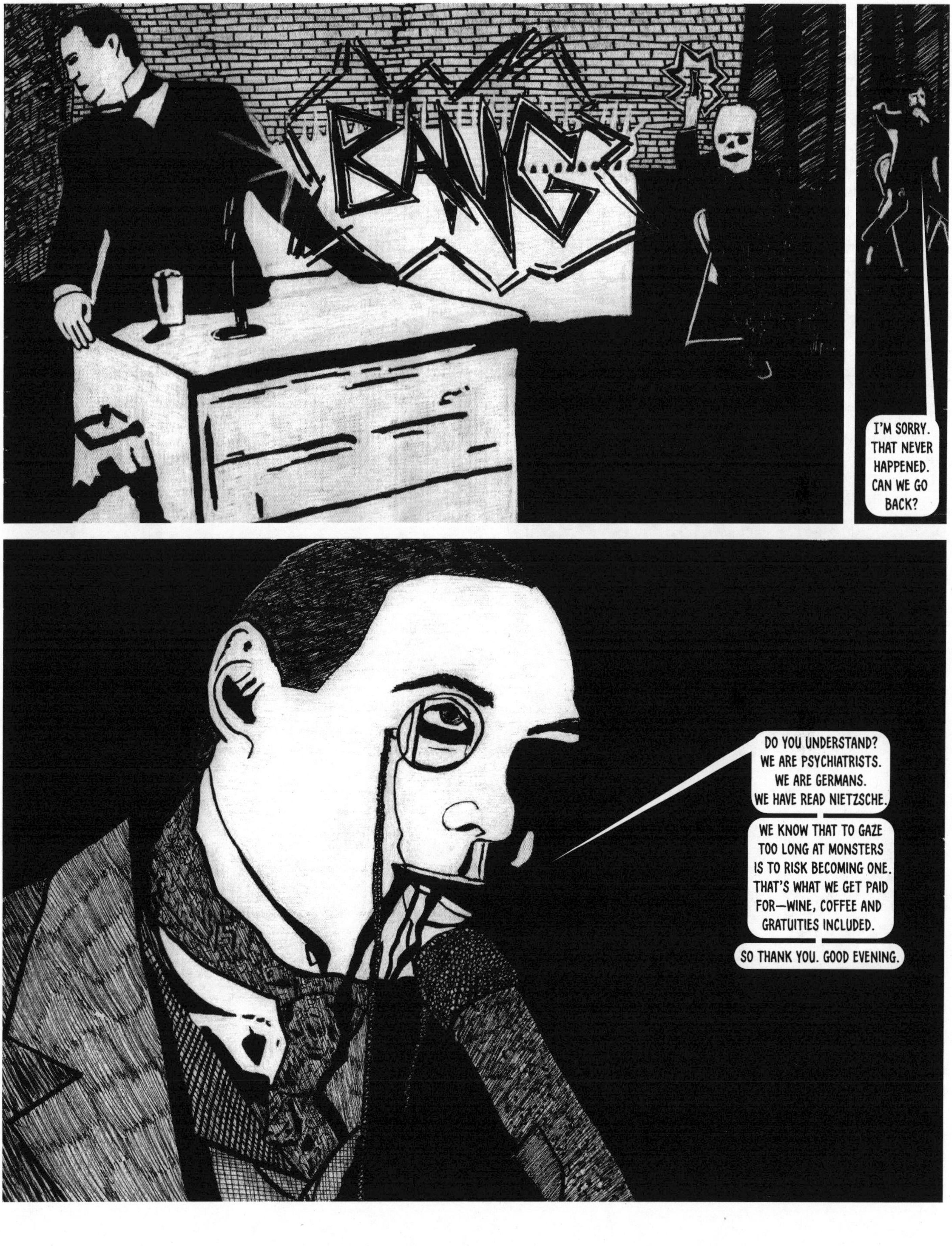
BANG
I'M SORRY. THAT NEVER HAPPENED. CAN WE GO BACK?
DO YOU UNDERSTAND? WE ARE PSYCHIATRISTS. WE ARE GERMANS. WE HAVE READ NIETZSCHE.
WE KNOW THAT TO GAZE TOO LONG AT MONSTERS IS TO RISK BECOMING ONE. THAT'S WHAT WE GET PAID FOR—WINE, COFFEE AND GRATUITIES INCLUDED.
SO THANK YOU. GOOD EVENING.

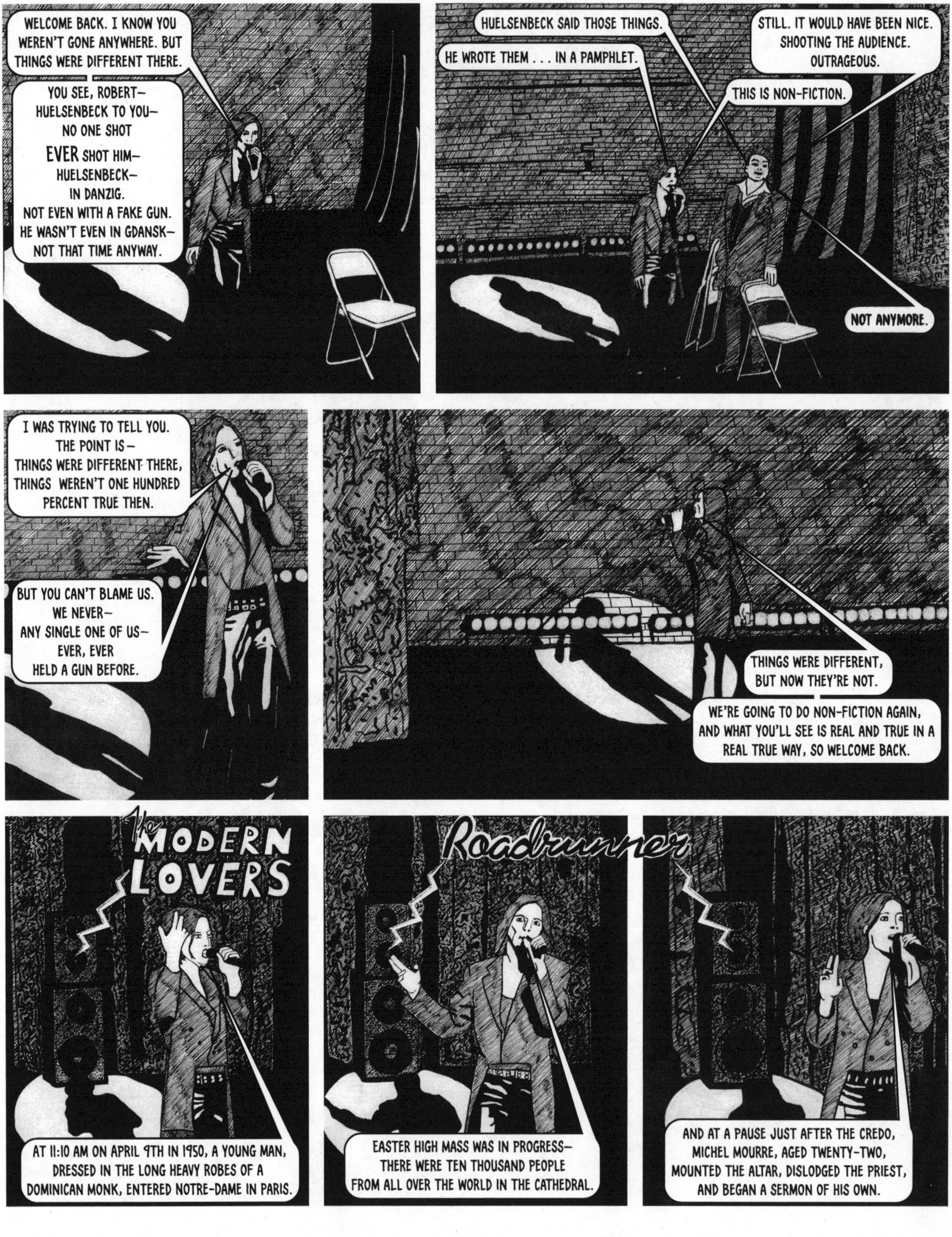
WELCOME BACK. I KNOW YOU WEREN'T GONE ANYWHERE. BUT THINGS WERE DIFFERENT THERE.
YOU SEE, ROBERT— HUELSENBECK TO YOU— NO ONE SHOT EVER SHOT HIM— HUELSENBECK— IN DANZIG. NOT EVEN WITH A FAKE GUN. HE WASN'T EVEN IN GDANSK— NOT THAT TIME ANYWAY.
HUELSENBECK SAID THOSE THINGS.
HE WROTE THEM . . . IN A PAMPHLET.
STILL. IT WOULD HAVE BEEN NICE. SHOOTING THE AUDIENCE. OUTRAGEOUS.
THIS IS NON-FICTION.
NOT ANYMORE.
I WAS TRYING TO TELL YOU. THE POINT IS— THINGS WERE DIFFERENT THERE, THINGS WEREN'T ONE HUNDRED PERCENT TRUE THEN.
BUT YOU CAN'T BLAME US. WE NEVER— ANY SINGLE ONE OF US— EVER, EVER HELD A GUN BEFORE.
THINGS WERE DIFFERENT, BUT NOW THEY'RE NOT.
WE'RE GOING TO DO NON-FICTION AGAIN, AND WHAT YOU'LL SEE IS REAL AND TRUE IN A REAL TRUE WAY, SO WELCOME BACK.
The MODERN LOVERS
Roadrunner
AT 11:10 AM ON APRIL 9TH IN 1950, A YOUNG MAN, DRESSED IN THE LONG HEAVY ROBES OF A DOMINICAN MONK, ENTERED NOTRE-DAME IN PARIS.
EASTER HIGH MASS WAS IN PROGRESS— THERE WERE TEN THOUSAND PEOPLE FROM ALL OVER THE WORLD IN THE CATHEDRAL.
AND AT A PAUSE JUST AFTER THE CREDO, MICHEL MOURRE, AGED TWENTY-TWO, MOUNTED THE ALTAR, DISLODGED THE PRIEST, AND BEGAN A SERMON OF HIS OWN.

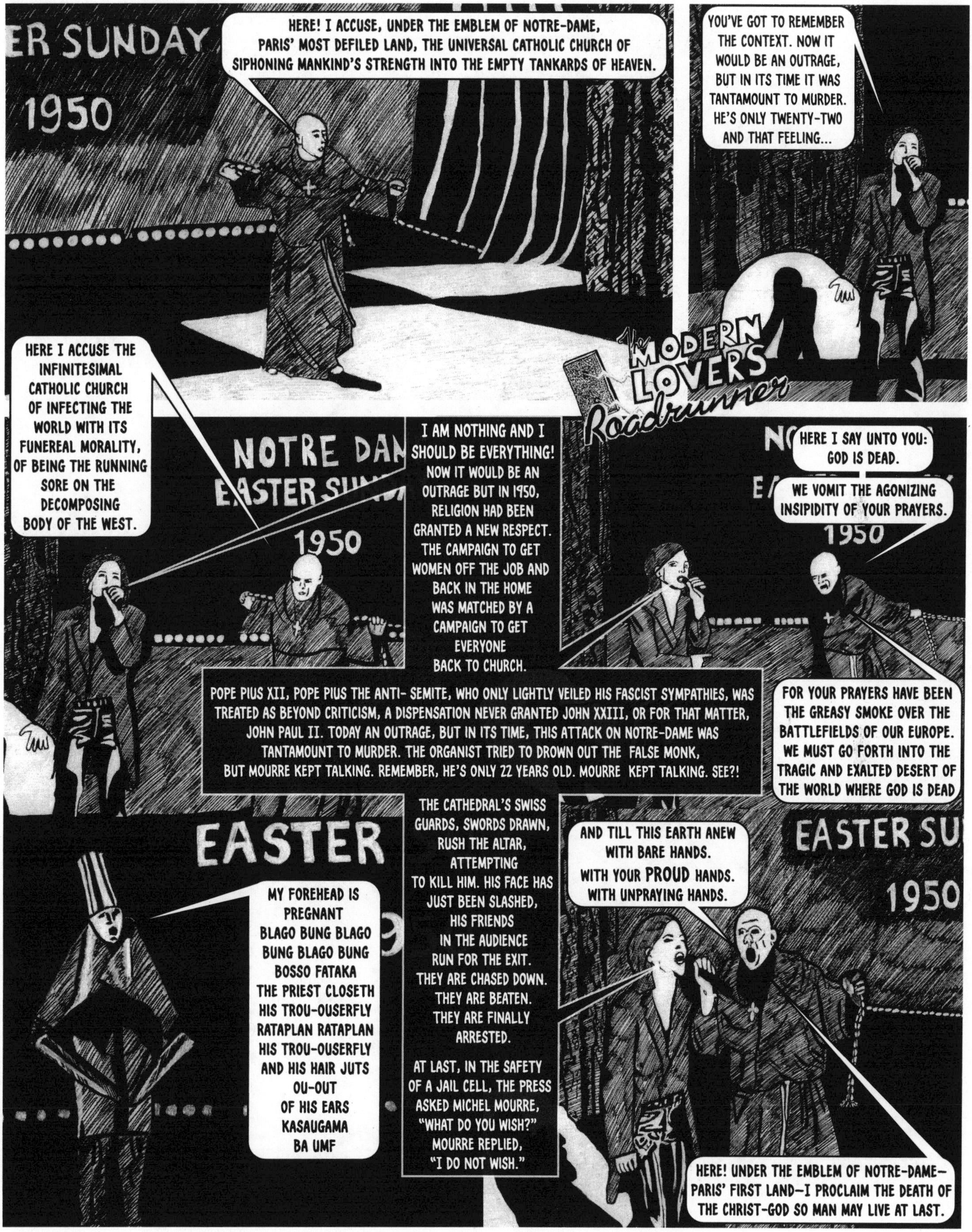
ER SUNDAY
1950
HERE! I ACCUSE, UNDER THE EMBLEM OF NOTRE-DAME, PARIS' MOST DEFILED LAND, THE UNIVERSAL CATHOLIC CHURCH OF SIPHONING MANKIND'S STRENGTH INTO THE EMPTY TANKARDS OF HEAVEN.
YOU'VE GOT TO REMEMBER THE CONTEXT. NOW IT WOULD BE AN OUTRAGE, BUT IN ITS TIME IT WAS TANTAMOUNT TO MURDER. HE'S ONLY TWENTY-TWO AND THAT FEELING...
The MODERN LOVERS Roadrunner
NOTRE DAM
EASTER SUN
1950
HERE I ACCUSE THE INFINITESIMAL CATHOLIC CHURCH OF INFECTING THE WORLD WITH ITS FUNEREAL MORALITY, OF BEING THE RUNNING SORE ON THE DECOMPOSING BODY OF THE WEST.
I AM NOTHING AND I SHOULD BE EVERYTHING! NOW IT WOULD BE AN OUTRAGE BUT IN 1950, RELIGION HAD BEEN GRANTED A NEW RESPECT. THE CAMPAIGN TO GET WOMEN OFF THE JOB AND BACK IN THE HOME WAS MATCHED BY A CAMPAIGN TO GET EVERYONE BACK TO CHURCH.
1950
HERE I SAY UNTO YOU: GOD IS DEAD.
WE VOMIT THE AGONIZING INSIPIDITY OF YOUR PRAYERS.
POPE PIUS XII, POPE PIUS THE ANTI- SEMITE, WHO ONLY LIGHTLY VEILED HIS FASCIST SYMPATHIES, WAS TREATED AS BEYOND CRITICISM, A DISPENSATION NEVER GRANTED JOHN XXIII, OR FOR THAT MATTER, JOHN PAUL II. TODAY AN OUTRAGE, BUT IN ITS TIME, THIS ATTACK ON NOTRE-DAME WAS TANTAMOUNT TO MURDER. THE ORGANIST TRIED TO DROWN OUT THE FALSE MONK, BUT MOURRE KEPT TALKING. REMEMBER, HE'S ONLY 22 YEARS OLD. MOURRE KEPT TALKING. SEE?!
FOR YOUR PRAYERS HAVE BEEN THE GREASY SMOKE OVER THE BATTLEFIELDS OF OUR EUROPE. WE MUST GO FORTH INTO THE TRAGIC AND EXALTED DESERT OF THE WORLD WHERE GOD IS DEAD
EASTER
MY FOREHEAD IS PREGNANT BLAGO BUNG BLAGO BUNG BLAGO BUNG BOSSO FATAKA THE PRIEST CLOSETH HIS TROU-OUSERFLY RATAPLAN RATAPLAN HIS TROU-OUSERFLY AND HIS HAIR JUTS OU-OUT OF HIS EARS KASAUGAMA BA UMF
THE CATHEDRAL'S SWISS GUARDS, SWORDS DRAWN, RUSH THE ALTAR, ATTEMPTING TO KILL HIM. HIS FACE HAS JUST BEEN SLASHED, HIS FRIENDS IN THE AUDIENCE RUN FOR THE EXIT. THEY ARE CHASED DOWN. THEY ARE BEATEN. THEY ARE FINALLY ARRESTED.
AT LAST, IN THE SAFETY OF A JAIL CELL, THE PRESS ASKED MICHEL MOURRE, "WHAT DO YOU WISH?" MOURRE REPLIED, "I DO NOT WISH."
EASTER SU
1950
AND TILL THIS EARTH ANEW WITH BARE HANDS. WITH YOUR PROUD HANDS. WITH UNPRAYING HANDS.
HERE! UNDER THE EMBLEM OF NOTRE-DAME—PARIS' FIRST LAND—I PROCLAIM THE DEATH OF THE CHRIST-GOD SO MAN MAY LIVE AT LAST.

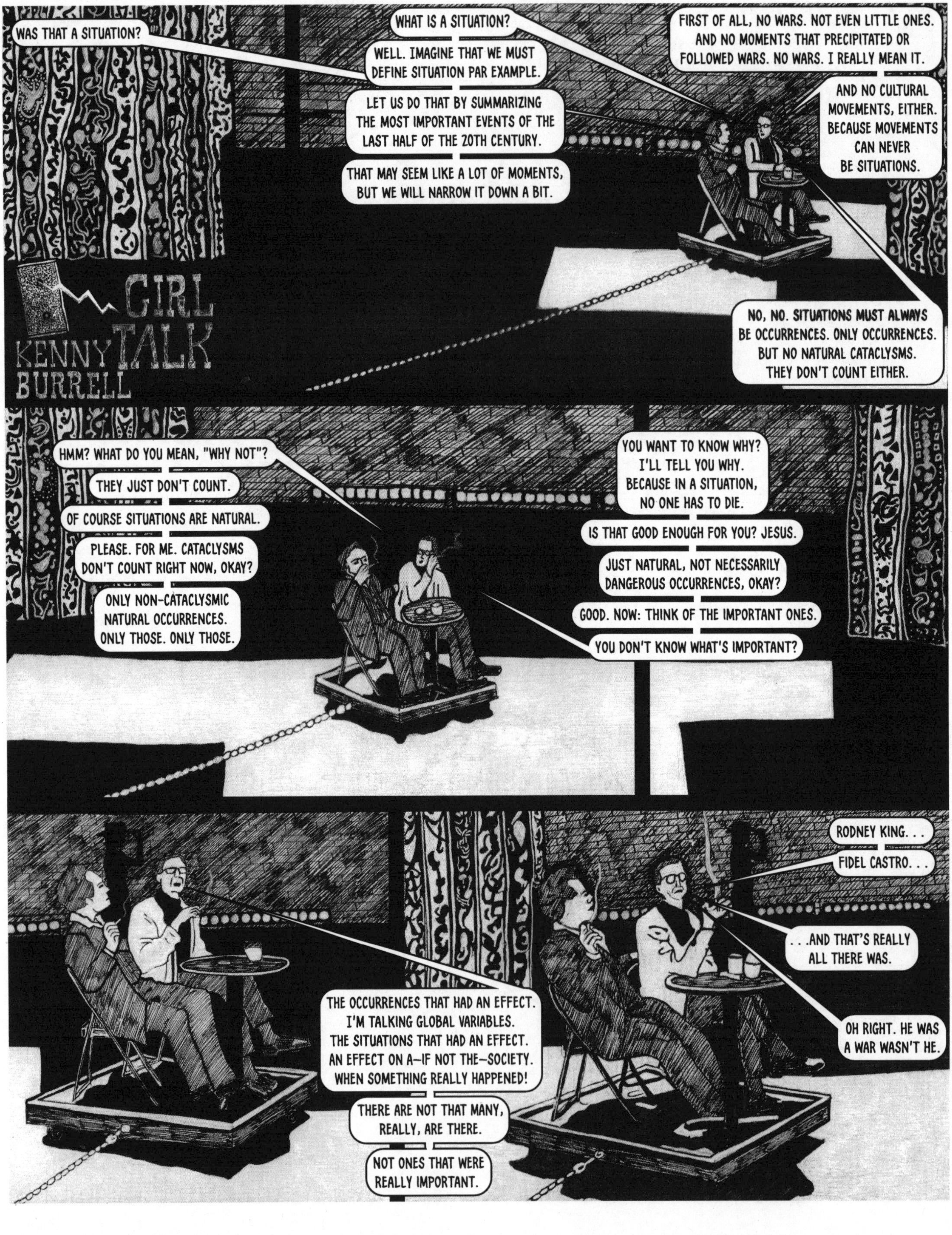
WAS THAT A SITUATION?
WHAT IS A SITUATION?
WELL. IMAGINE THAT WE MUST DEFINE SITUATION PAR EXAMPLE.
LET US DO THAT BY SUMMARIZING THE MOST IMPORTANT EVENTS OF THE LAST HALF OF THE 20TH CENTURY.
THAT MAY SEEM LIKE A LOT OF MOMENTS, BUT WE WILL NARROW IT DOWN A BIT.
FIRST OF ALL, NO WARS. NOT EVEN LITTLE ONES. AND NO MOMENTS THAT PRECIPITATED OR FOLLOWED WARS. NO WARS. I REALLY MEAN IT.
AND NO CULTURAL MOVEMENTS, EITHER. BECAUSE MOVEMENTS CAN NEVER BE SITUATIONS.
GIRL TALK
KENNY BURRELL
NO, NO. SITUATIONS MUST ALWAYS BE OCCURRENCES. ONLY OCCURRENCES. BUT NO NATURAL CATACLYSMS. THEY DON'T COUNT EITHER.
HMM? WHAT DO YOU MEAN, "WHY NOT"?
THEY JUST DON'T COUNT.
OF COURSE SITUATIONS ARE NATURAL.
PLEASE. FOR ME. CATACLYSMS DON'T COUNT RIGHT NOW, OKAY?
ONLY NON-CATACLYSMIC NATURAL OCCURRENCES. ONLY THOSE. ONLY THOSE.
YOU WANT TO KNOW WHY? I'LL TELL YOU WHY. BECAUSE IN A SITUATION, NO ONE HAS TO DIE.
IS THAT GOOD ENOUGH FOR YOU? JESUS.
JUST NATURAL, NOT NECESSARILY DANGEROUS OCCURRENCES, OKAY?
GOOD. NOW: THINK OF THE IMPORTANT ONES.
YOU DON'T KNOW WHAT'S IMPORTANT?
THE OCCURRENCES THAT HAD AN EFFECT. I'M TALKING GLOBAL VARIABLES. THE SITUATIONS THAT HAD AN EFFECT. AN EFFECT ON A—IF NOT THE—SOCIETY. WHEN SOMETHING REALLY HAPPENED!
THERE ARE NOT THAT MANY, REALLY, ARE THERE.
NOT ONES THAT WERE REALLY IMPORTANT.
RODNEY KING. . .
FIDEL CASTRO. . .
. . .AND THAT'S REALLY ALL THERE WAS.
OH RIGHT. HE WAS A WAR WASN'T HE.

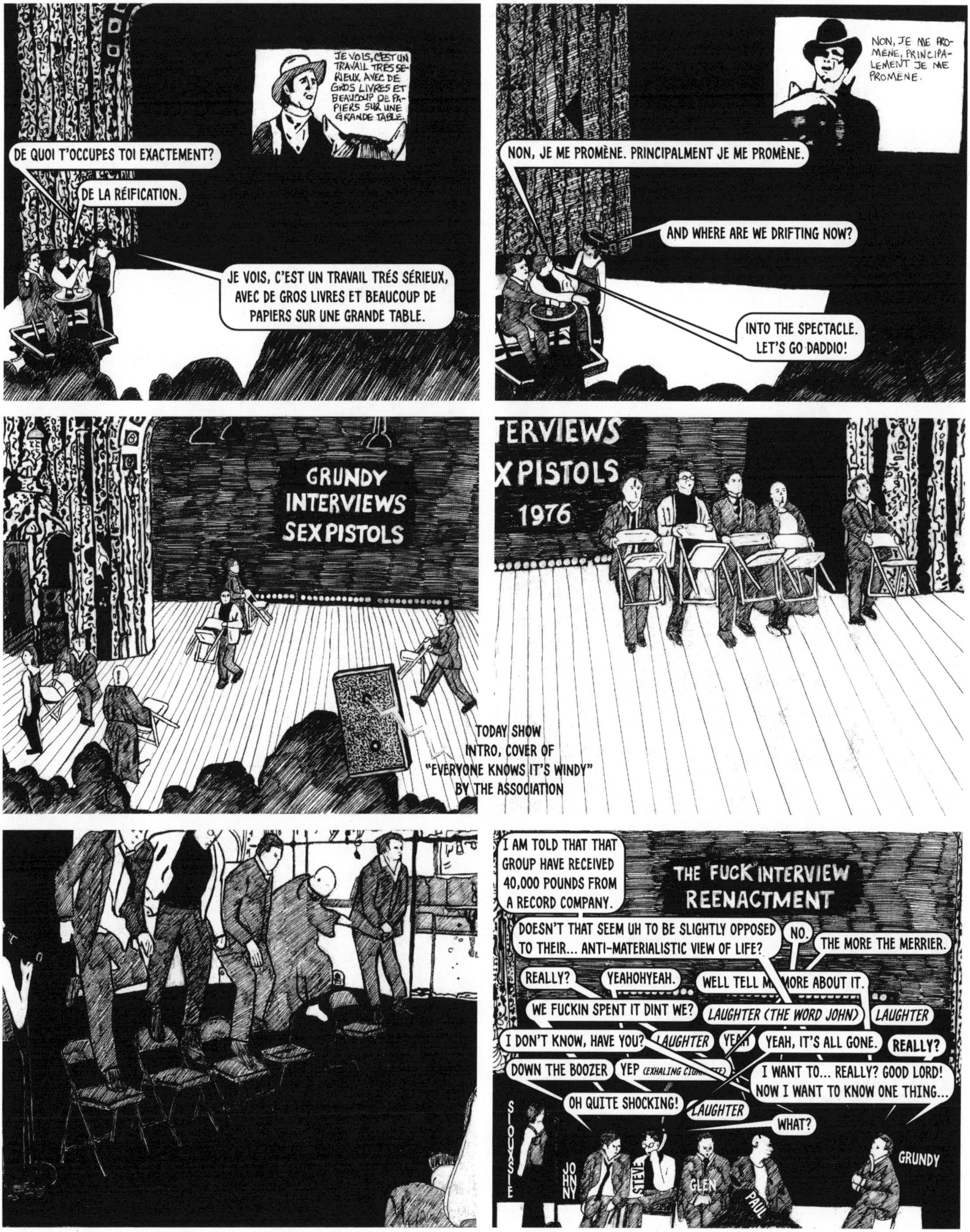

JE VOIS, C'EST UN TRAVAIL TRÉS SÉRIEUX, AVEC DE GROS LIVRES ET BEAUCOUP DE PAPIERS SUR UNE GRANDE TABLE.
DE QUOI T'OCCUPES TOI EXACTEMENT?
DE LA RÉIFICATION.
JE VOIS, C'EST UN TRAVAIL TRÉS SÉRIEUX, AVEC DE GROS LIVRES ET BEAUCOUP DE PAPIERS SUR UNE GRANDE TABLE.
NON, JE ME PROMÈNE, PRINCIPALEMENT JE ME PROMÈNE.
NON, JE ME PROMÈNE. PRINCIPALMENT JE ME PROMÈNE.
AND WHERE ARE WE DRIFTING NOW?
INTO THE SPECTACLE. LET'S GO DADDIO!
GRUNDY INTERVIEWS SEX PISTOLS
TODAY SHOW INTRO, COVER OF "EVERYONE KNOWS IT'S WINDY" BY THE ASSOCIATION
TERVIEWS
X PISTOLS
1976
THE "FUCK" INTERVIEW REENACTMENT
I AM TOLD THAT THAT GROUP HAVE RECEIVED 40,000 POUNDS FROM A RECORD COMPANY.
DOESN'T THAT SEEM UH TO BE SLIGHTLY OPPOSED TO THEIR... ANTI-MATERIALISTIC VIEW OF LIFE?
NO.
THE MORE THE MERRIER.
REALLY?
YEAHOHYEAH.
WELL TELL M MORE ABOUT IT.
WE FUCKIN SPENT IT DINT WE?
LAUGHTER (THE WORD JOHN)
LAUGHTER
I DON'T KNOW, HAVE YOU?
LAUGHTER
YE
YEAH, IT'S ALL GONE.
REALLY?
DOWN THE BOOZER
YEP (EXHALING CIG
I WANT TO... REALLY? GOOD LORD! NOW I WANT TO KNOW ONE THING...
OH QUITE SHOCKING!
LAUGHTER
WHAT?
SIOUXSIE
JOHNNY
STEVE
GLEN
PAUL
GRUNDY

GRUNDY: ARE YOU SERIOUS OR ARE YOU JUST MAKING IT... TRYING TO MAKE ME LAUGH.
    GLEN: YES.   IT'S GONE, GONE.
GRUNDY: REALLY?
GLEN: YEAH.
GRUNDY: NO BUT I MEAN ABOUT WHAT YOU'RE DOING.
GLEN: OH YEAH.
GRUNDY: Y- YOU ARE SERIOUS.
GLEN: MM.
GRUNDY: BEETHOVEN, MOZART, BACH, BRAHMS, HAVE ALL DIED . . .
   JOHNNY: OH YES THEY'RE ALL HEROES OF OURS, AIN'T THEY.

GRUNDY: REALLY, WH-WH-GO-WHAT ARE YOU SAYING SIR?
       JOHNNY: YES. THEY'RE ALL WOONNDERFUL PEOPLE.
GRUNDY: ARE THEY?
JOHNNY: OH YES. THEY REALLY TURN US ON.
         PAUL: LAUGHTER
STEVE: *(DEEP, SARCASTIC VOICE)* BUT THEY'RE DEAD.
GRUNDY: WELL SUPPOSE THEY TURN OTHER PEOPLE ON?
PAUL: *LAUGHTER*
JOHNNY: *(QUIETLY)* THAT'S JUST THEIR TOUGH SHIT.
GRUNDY: IT'S WHAT?

JOHNNY: NOTHING. A RUDE WORD. NEXT QUESTION.
      PAUL: *(SOUND OF A CIGARETTE EXHALE.)*
GRUNDY: NONO. WHAT WAS THE RUDE WORD?
JOHNNY: SHIT.
GRUNDY: WAS IT REALLY?! GOOD HEAVENS YOU FRIGHTEN ME TO DEATH.
     JOHNNY: OHHH RIGHT . . . SO YOU WANT TO PLAY GAMES YOU ROARING PRISS.
          GLEN: HE'S LIKE YOUR DAD INT HE THIS GEEZER...
GRUNDY: WHAT ABOUT YOU GIRLS BEHIND . . .
GLEN: YOUR GRANDAD.
        PAUL: LAUGHTER
GRUNDY: *(TO GIRLS)* ARE YOU UH . . . ARE YOU WORRIED?
       OR YOU JUST ENJOYING YOURSELVES.
SIOUXSIE: ENJOYING MYSELF.
GRUNDY: ARE YOU?
SIOUXSIE: YEAH.
GURNDY: AH, THAT'S WHAT I THOUGHT YOU WERE DOING.
      PAUL: *(SOUND OF CIGARETTE EXHALE.)*
SIOUXSIE: I ALWAYS WANTED TO MEET YOU.
GRUNDY: DID YOU REALLY?
SIOUXSIE: YEAH.

GRUNDY: WE'LL MEET AFTERWARDS, SHALL WE?
ALL PUNKS: *LAUGHTER*
STEVE: YOU DIRTY SOD. (LAUGHING) YOU DIRTY OLD MAN.
ALL PUNKS: *LAUGHTER*
STEVE: YOU DIRTY OLD MAN.
GRUNDY: WELL KEEP GOING, CHIEF.   KEEP GOING.
      GLEN: *LAUGHTER.*
GRUNDY: GO ON. YOU'VE GOT ANOTHER 5 SECONDS, SAY SOMETHING OUTRAGEOUS.
           STEVE: YOU DIR . . .
STEVE: YOU DIRTY BASTARD.
PAUL: *LAUGHTER*
GRUNDY: GO ON. AGAIN.
STEVE: YOU DIRTY FUCKER.   ALL PUNKS: *LAUGHTER*
GRUNDY: WHAT A CLEVER BOY!
STEVE: WHAT A FUCKING ROTTER.
GRUNDY: WELL THAT'S IT FOR TONIGHT. THE OTHER "ROCKER" – EAMONN –
       AND I'LL SAY NOTHING ELSE ABOUT HIM, WILL BE BACK TOMORROW.
       (TO CAMERA) I'LL BE SEEING YOU SOON,
       (TO PISTOLS) I HOPE I'M NOT SEEING YOU AGAIN.
       FROM ME THOUGH, GOOD NIGHT.

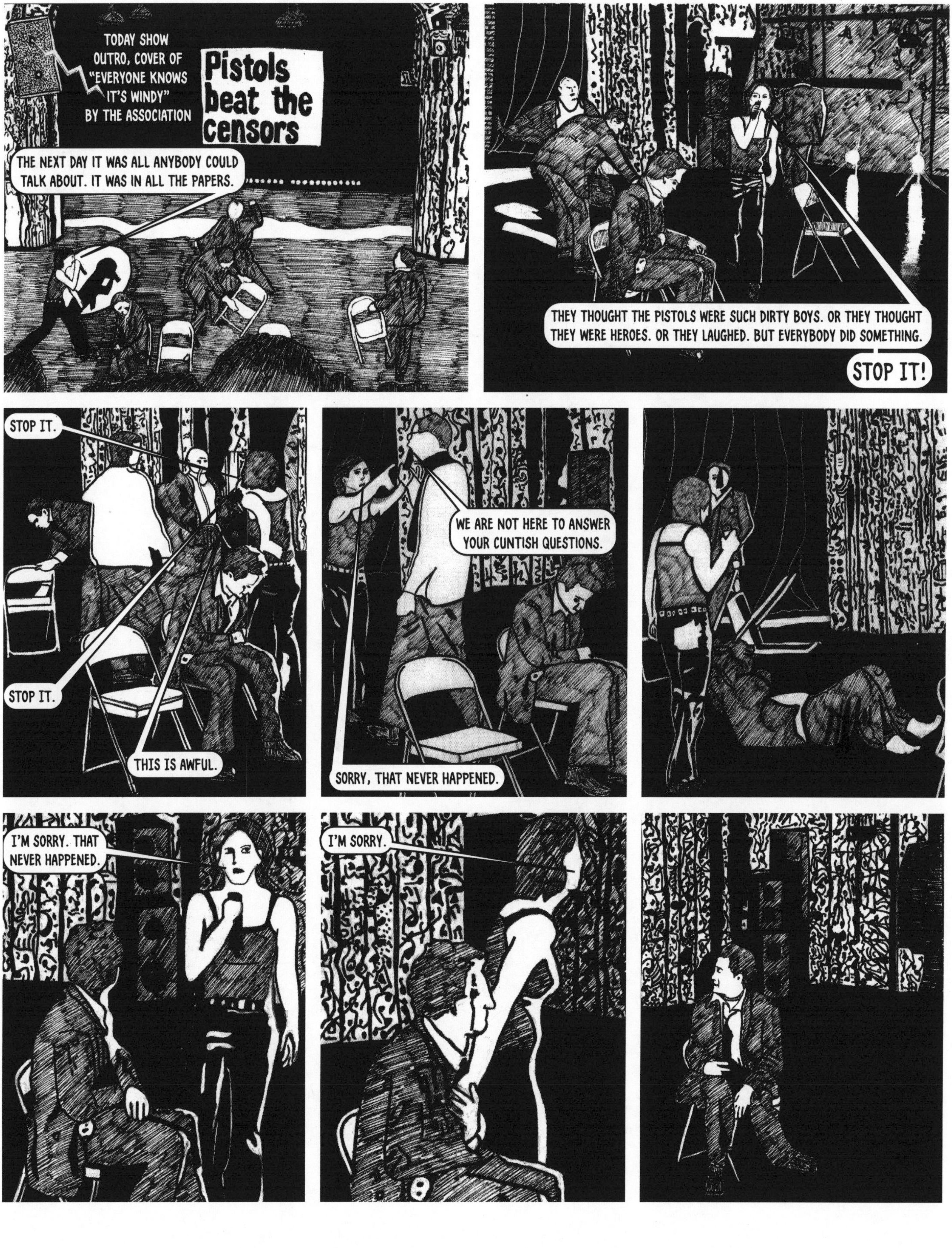
TODAY SHOW
OUTRO, COVER OF
"EVERYONE KNOWS
IT'S WINDY"
BY THE ASSOCIATION
Pistols beat the censors
THE NEXT DAY IT WAS ALL ANYBODY COULD TALK ABOUT. IT WAS IN ALL THE PAPERS.
THEY THOUGHT THE PISTOLS WERE SUCH DIRTY BOYS. OR THEY THOUGHT THEY WERE HEROES. OR THEY LAUGHED. BUT EVERYBODY DID SOMETHING.
STOP IT!
STOP IT.
STOP IT.
THIS IS AWFUL.
WE ARE NOT HERE TO ANSWER YOUR CUNTISH QUESTIONS.
SORRY, THAT NEVER HAPPENED.
I'M SORRY. THAT NEVER HAPPENED.
I'M SORRY.

A LOT HAS BEEN WRITTEN AND SAID ABOUT PUNK AND THE SEX PISTOLS. MOST OF IT HAS BEEN EITHER SENSATIONALISM OR JOURNALISTIC PSYCHOBABBLE.

THE REST HAS BEEN MERE SPITE.

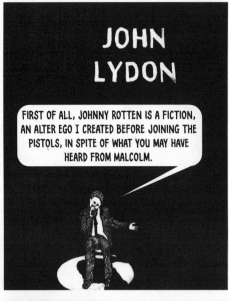

JOHN LYDON

FIRST OF ALL, JOHNNY ROTTEN IS A FICTION, AN ALTER EGO I CREATED BEFORE JOINING THE PISTOLS, IN SPITE OF WHAT YOU MAY HAVE HEARD FROM MALCOLM.

IF YOU MISSED THAT ALONG THE WAY, DON'T WORRY TOO MUCH ABOUT IT. SID DIDN'T GET IT EITHER AND HE WAS IN THE FUCKING BAND WITH ME.

I'M A SPITEFUL BASTARD. I ALWAYS HAVE BEEN.

I WAS APPARENTLY BORN IN LONDON. I'M NOT SO SURE. FOR SOME REASON MY BIRTH CERTIFICATE WAS ISSUED TWO YEARS AFTER I WAS BORN.

MY IRISH HALF PROVIDED MY SENSE OF DEVILRY.

LIKE... OSCAR WILDE, MY PHILOSOPHY IS JUST GO AND SEE WHAT YOU CAN CAUSE.

IF I HAD TO CARICATURE MYSELF, THE CLOSEST I'VE SEEN TO IT WOULD BE LAURENCE OLIVIER'S RICHARD III. I CAN SEE BITS OF ME IN THERE.

BENEATH HIS HUNCHED DEFORMITY, SHAKESPEARE'S RICHARD WAS WICKED AND PSYCHOTIC—OLIVIER'S RICHARD WAS RIVETING IN HIS EXCESSIVE DISGUST.

I TOOK INFLUENCES FROM THIS PERFORMANCE WHEN I CONCEIVED ROTTEN. I HAD NEVER SEEN A POP SINGER PRESENT HIMSELF IN QUITE THIS MANNER.

YOU'RE SUPPOSED TO BE A NICE PRETTY BOY, SING LOVELY SONGS, AND COO AT THE GIRLIES.

RICHARD III WOULD HAVE NONE OF THAT.

HE GOT THE GIRLS IN OTHER WAYS.

STAGE PERSONAS ARE ONE THING, BUT I HAVE NO TIME FOR LIES OR FANTASY!

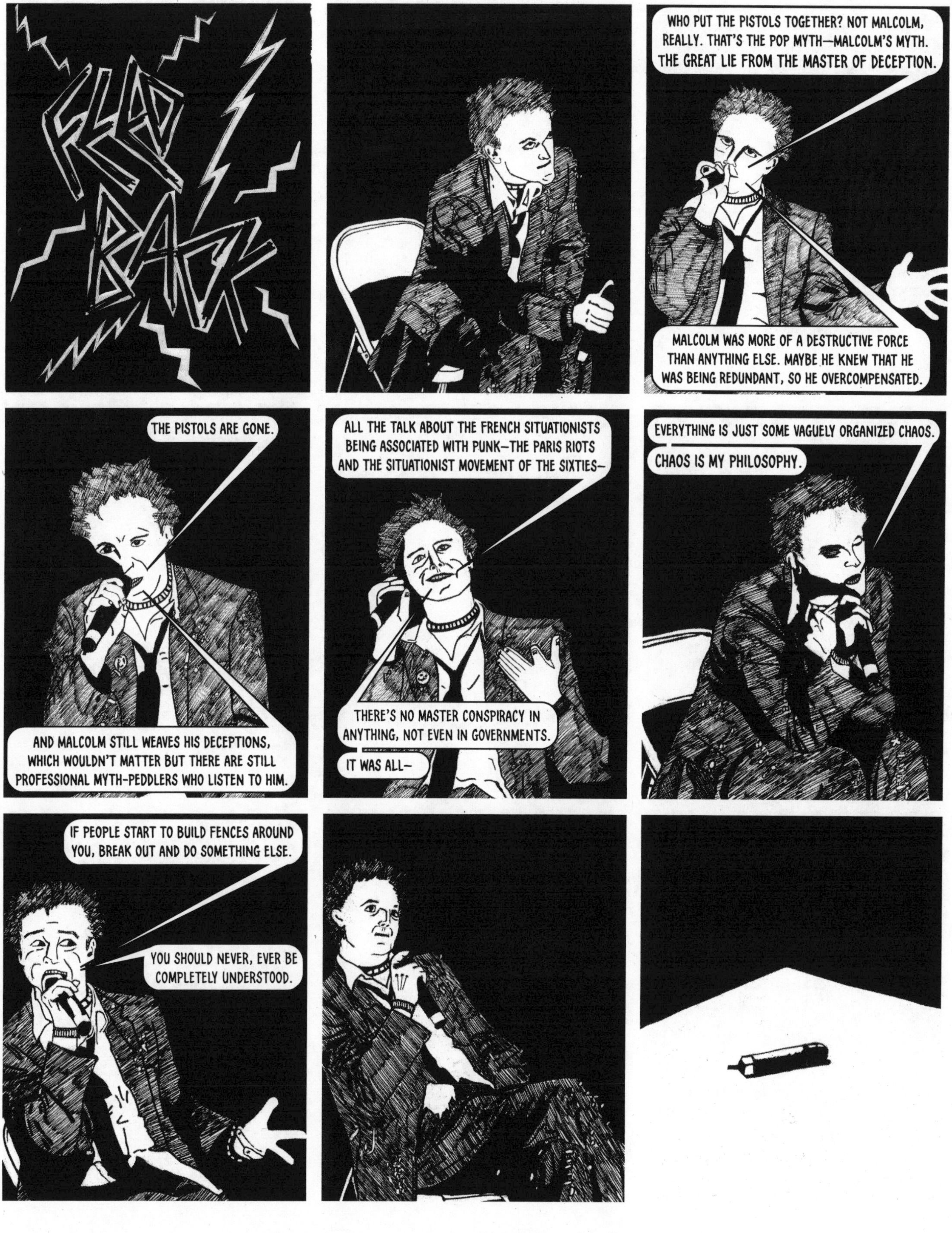
WHO PUT THE PISTOLS TOGETHER? NOT MALCOLM, REALLY. THAT'S THE POP MYTH—MALCOLM'S MYTH. THE GREAT LIE FROM THE MASTER OF DECEPTION.
MALCOLM WAS MORE OF A DESTRUCTIVE FORCE THAN ANYTHING ELSE. MAYBE HE KNEW THAT HE WAS BEING REDUNDANT, SO HE OVERCOMPENSATED.
THE PISTOLS ARE GONE.
AND MALCOLM STILL WEAVES HIS DECEPTIONS, WHICH WOULDN'T MATTER BUT THERE ARE STILL PROFESSIONAL MYTH-PEDDLERS WHO LISTEN TO HIM.
ALL THE TALK ABOUT THE FRENCH SITUATIONISTS BEING ASSOCIATED WITH PUNK—THE PARIS RIOTS AND THE SITUATIONIST MOVEMENT OF THE SIXTIES—
THERE'S NO MASTER CONSPIRACY IN ANYTHING, NOT EVEN IN GOVERNMENTS.
IT WAS ALL—
EVERYTHING IS JUST SOME VAGUELY ORGANIZED CHAOS.
CHAOS IS MY PHILOSOPHY.
IF PEOPLE START TO BUILD FENCES AROUND YOU, BREAK OUT AND DO SOMETHING ELSE.
YOU SHOULD NEVER, EVER BE COMPLETELY UNDERSTOOD.

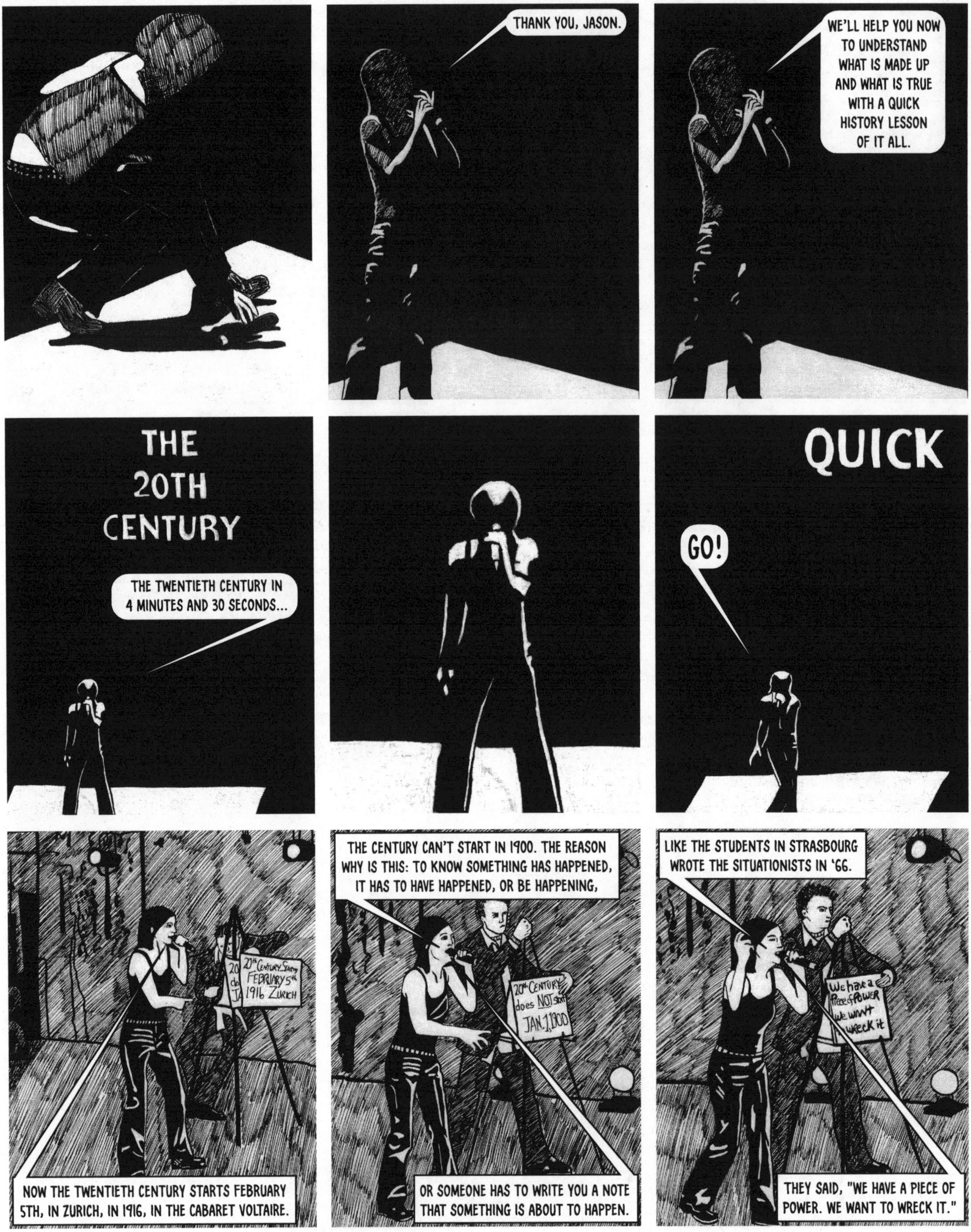
THANK YOU, JASON.
WE'LL HELP YOU NOW TO UNDERSTAND WHAT IS MADE UP AND WHAT IS TRUE WITH A QUICK HISTORY LESSON OF IT ALL.
THE 20TH CENTURY
THE TWENTIETH CENTURY IN 4 MINUTES AND 30 SECONDS...
QUICK
GO!
FEBRUARY 5th 1916 ZURICH
NOW THE TWENTIETH CENTURY STARTS FEBRUARY 5TH, IN ZURICH, IN 1916, IN THE CABARET VOLTAIRE.
THE CENTURY CAN'T START IN 1900. THE REASON WHY IS THIS: TO KNOW SOMETHING HAS HAPPENED, IT HAS TO HAVE HAPPENED, OR BE HAPPENING,
20th CENTURY does NOT start JAN. 1, 1900
OR SOMEONE HAS TO WRITE YOU A NOTE THAT SOMETHING IS ABOUT TO HAPPEN.
LIKE THE STUDENTS IN STRASBOURG WROTE THE SITUATIONISTS IN '66.
We have a Piece of POWER we want wreck it
THEY SAID, "WE HAVE A PIECE OF POWER. WE WANT TO WRECK IT."

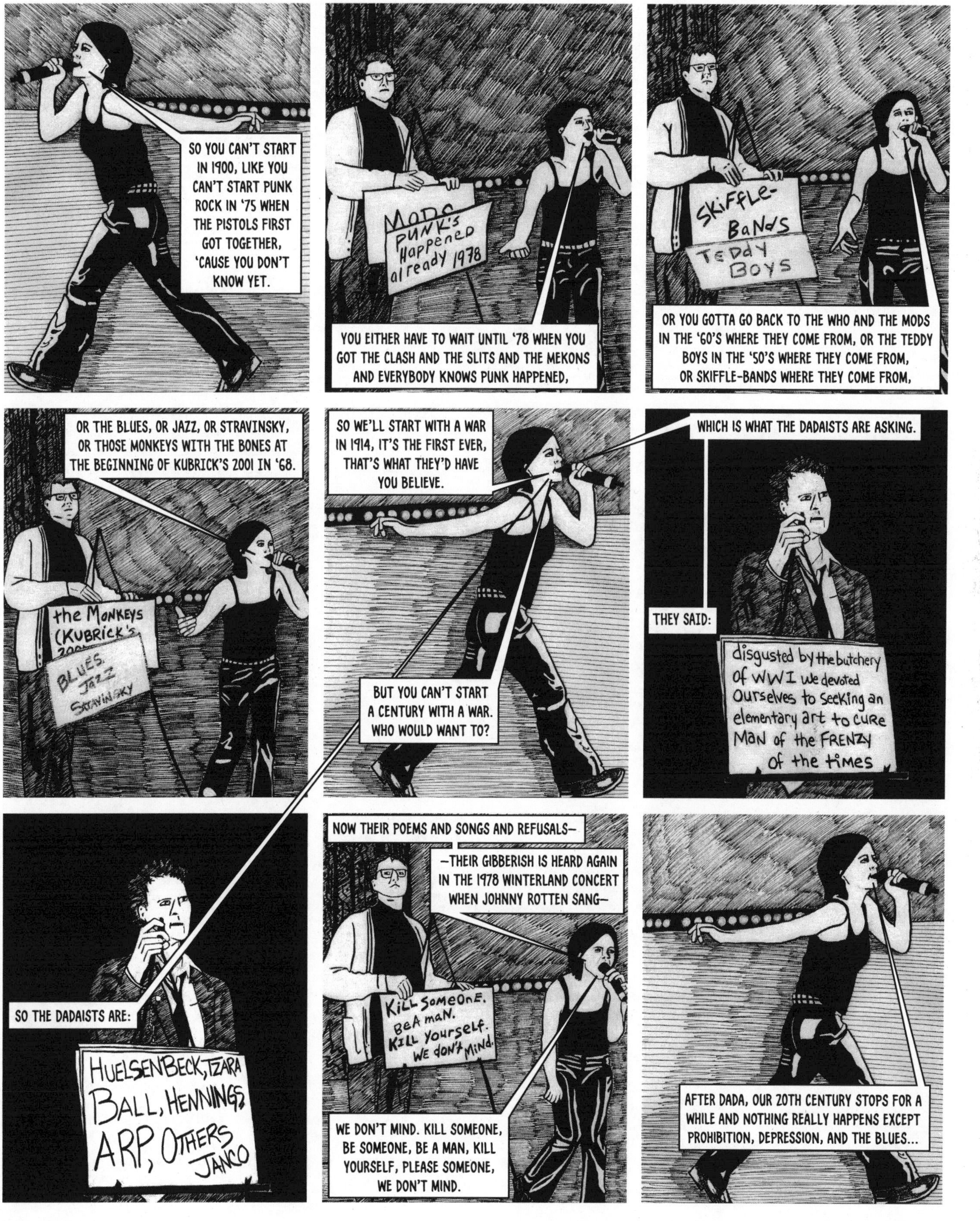
SO YOU CAN'T START IN 1900, LIKE YOU CAN'T START PUNK ROCK IN '75 WHEN THE PISTOLS FIRST GOT TOGETHER, 'CAUSE YOU DON'T KNOW YET.
MODS
PUNK'S Happened already 1978
YOU EITHER HAVE TO WAIT UNTIL '78 WHEN YOU GOT THE CLASH AND THE SLITS AND THE MEKONS AND EVERYBODY KNOWS PUNK HAPPENED,
SKIFFLE-BANDS
TEDDY BOYS
OR YOU GOTTA GO BACK TO THE WHO AND THE MODS IN THE '60'S WHERE THEY COME FROM, OR THE TEDDY BOYS IN THE '50'S WHERE THEY COME FROM, OR SKIFFLE-BANDS WHERE THEY COME FROM,
OR THE BLUES, OR JAZZ, OR STRAVINSKY, OR THOSE MONKEYS WITH THE BONES AT THE BEGINNING OF KUBRICK'S 2001 IN '68.
the Monkeys (KUBRICK'S
BLUES JAZZ STRAVINSKY
SO WE'LL START WITH A WAR IN 1914, IT'S THE FIRST EVER, THAT'S WHAT THEY'D HAVE YOU BELIEVE.
BUT YOU CAN'T START A CENTURY WITH A WAR. WHO WOULD WANT TO?
WHICH IS WHAT THE DADAISTS ARE ASKING.
THEY SAID:
disgusted by the butchery of WWI we devoted ourselves to seeking an elementary art to cure Man of the FRENZY of the times
SO THE DADAISTS ARE:
HUELSENBECK, TZARA BALL, HENNINGS, ARP, OTHERS JANCO
NOW THEIR POEMS AND SONGS AND REFUSALS—
—THEIR GIBBERISH IS HEARD AGAIN IN THE 1978 WINTERLAND CONCERT WHEN JOHNNY ROTTEN SANG—
KILL SOMEONE. BE A MAN. KILL yourself. We don't Mind.
WE DON'T MIND. KILL SOMEONE, BE SOMEONE, BE A MAN, KILL YOURSELF, PLEASE SOMEONE, WE DON'T MIND.
AFTER DADA, OUR 20TH CENTURY STOPS FOR A WHILE AND NOTHING REALLY HAPPENS EXCEPT PROHIBITION, DEPRESSION, AND THE BLUES...

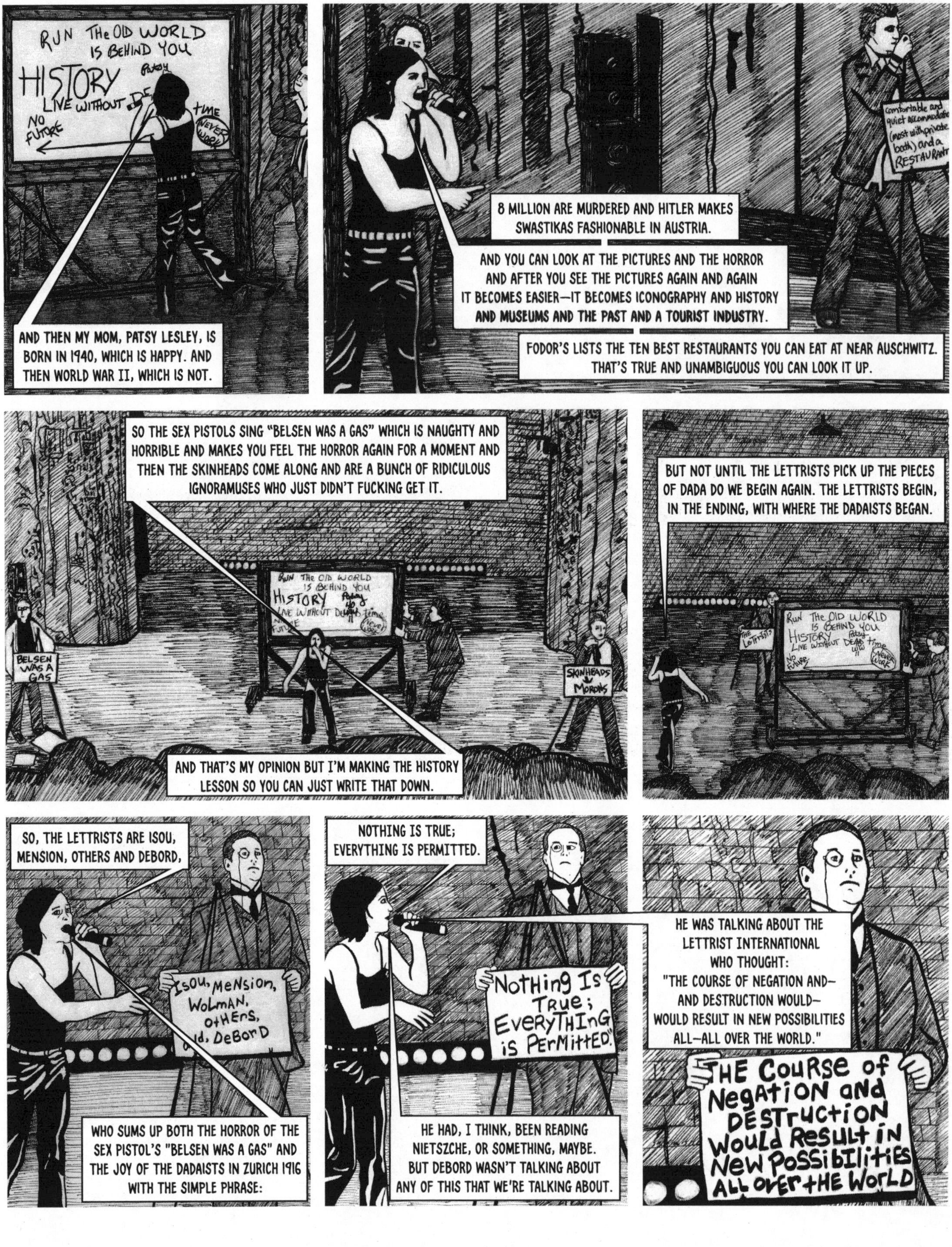
RUN THE OLD WORLD IS BEHIND YOU
HISTORY
NO FUTURE
time
NEVER WORK
AND THEN MY MOM, PATSY LESLEY, IS BORN IN 1940, WHICH IS HAPPY. AND THEN WORLD WAR II, WHICH IS NOT.
comfortable and quiet accommodation (most with private bath) and a RESTAURANT
8 MILLION ARE MURDERED AND HITLER MAKES SWASTIKAS FASHIONABLE IN AUSTRIA.
AND YOU CAN LOOK AT THE PICTURES AND THE HORROR AND AFTER YOU SEE THE PICTURES AGAIN AND AGAIN IT BECOMES EASIER—IT BECOMES ICONOGRAPHY AND HISTORY AND MUSEUMS AND THE PAST AND A TOURIST INDUSTRY.
FODOR'S LISTS THE TEN BEST RESTAURANTS YOU CAN EAT AT NEAR AUSCHWITZ. THAT'S TRUE AND UNAMBIGUOUS YOU CAN LOOK IT UP.
SO THE SEX PISTOLS SING "BELSEN WAS A GAS" WHICH IS NAUGHTY AND HORRIBLE AND MAKES YOU FEEL THE HORROR AGAIN FOR A MOMENT AND THEN THE SKINHEADS COME ALONG AND ARE A BUNCH OF RIDICULOUS IGNORAMUSES WHO JUST DIDN'T FUCKING GET IT.
BELSEN WAS A GAS
SKINHEADS MORONS
AND THAT'S MY OPINION BUT I'M MAKING THE HISTORY LESSON SO YOU CAN JUST WRITE THAT DOWN.
BUT NOT UNTIL THE LETTRISTS PICK UP THE PIECES OF DADA DO WE BEGIN AGAIN. THE LETTRISTS BEGIN, IN THE ENDING, WITH WHERE THE DADAISTS BEGAN.
THE LETTRISTS
SO, THE LETTRISTS ARE ISOU, MENSION, OTHERS AND DEBORD,
ISOU, MENSION, WOLMAN, OTHERS, DEBORD
WHO SUMS UP BOTH THE HORROR OF THE SEX PISTOL'S "BELSEN WAS A GAS" AND THE JOY OF THE DADAISTS IN ZURICH 1916 WITH THE SIMPLE PHRASE:
NOTHING IS TRUE; EVERYTHING IS PERMITTED.
NOTHING IS TRUE; EVERYTHING IS PERMITTED.
HE HAD, I THINK, BEEN READING NIETSZCHE, OR SOMETHING, MAYBE. BUT DEBORD WASN'T TALKING ABOUT ANY OF THIS THAT WE'RE TALKING ABOUT.
HE WAS TALKING ABOUT THE LETTRIST INTERNATIONAL WHO THOUGHT: "THE COURSE OF NEGATION AND—AND DESTRUCTION WOULD—WOULD RESULT IN NEW POSSIBILITIES ALL—ALL OVER THE WORLD."
THE COURSE OF NEGATION AND DESTRUCTION WOULD RESULT IN NEW POSSIBILITIES ALL OVER THE WORLD

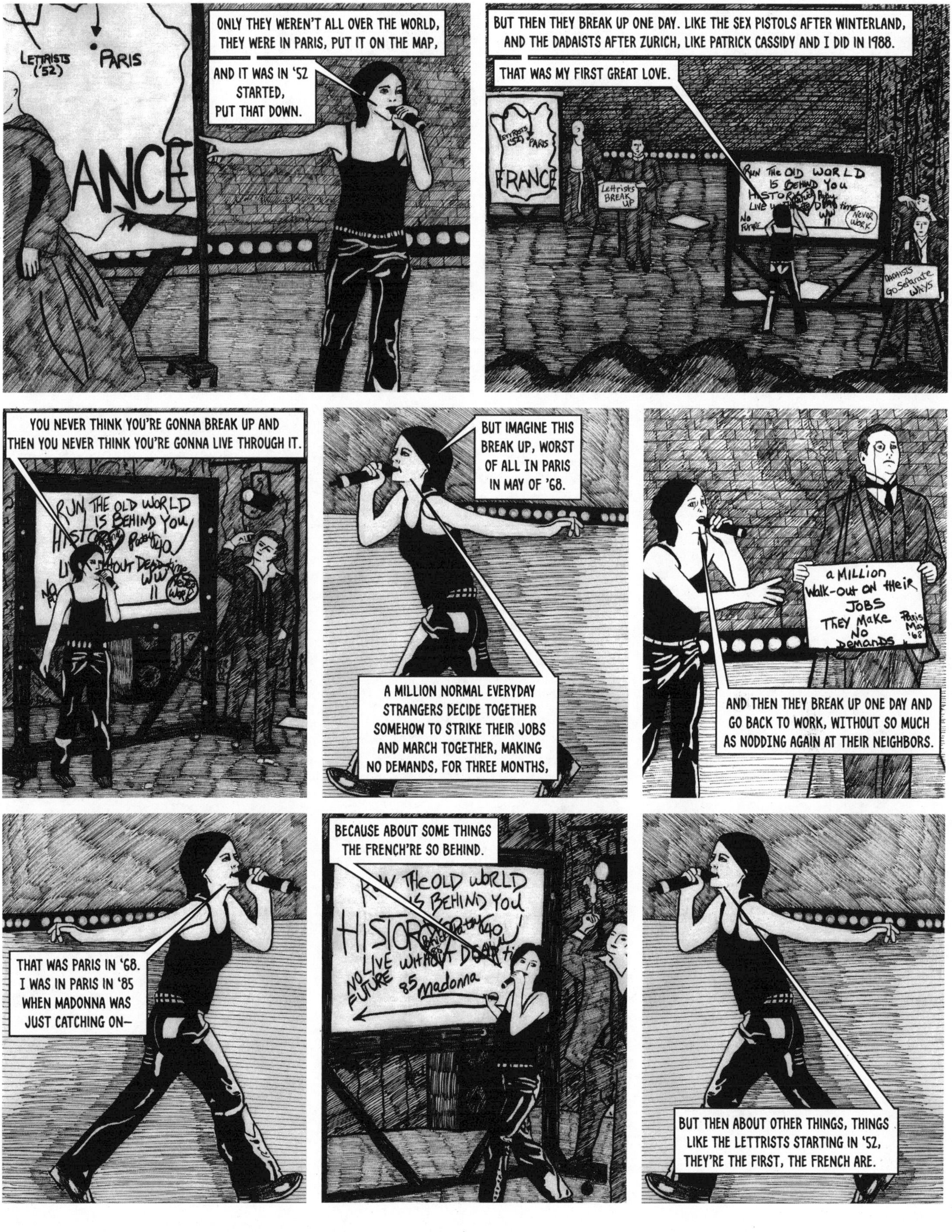
LETTRISTS ('52)
PARIS
ANCE
ONLY THEY WEREN'T ALL OVER THE WORLD, THEY WERE IN PARIS, PUT IT ON THE MAP,
AND IT WAS IN '52 STARTED, PUT THAT DOWN.
BUT THEN THEY BREAK UP ONE DAY. LIKE THE SEX PISTOLS AFTER WINTERLAND, AND THE DADAISTS AFTER ZURICH, LIKE PATRICK CASSIDY AND I DID IN 1988.
THAT WAS MY FIRST GREAT LOVE.
FRANCE
Lettrists BREAK UP
RUN THE OLD WORLD IS BEHIND YOU
NO FUTURE
NEVER WORK
DADAISTS GO SEPARATE WAYS
YOU NEVER THINK YOU'RE GONNA BREAK UP AND THEN YOU NEVER THINK YOU'RE GONNA LIVE THROUGH IT.
RUN THE OLD WORLD IS BEHIND YOU
BUT IMAGINE THIS BREAK UP, WORST OF ALL IN PARIS IN MAY OF '68.
A MILLION NORMAL EVERYDAY STRANGERS DECIDE TOGETHER SOMEHOW TO STRIKE THEIR JOBS AND MARCH TOGETHER, MAKING NO DEMANDS, FOR THREE MONTHS,
a MILLION Walk-out on their JOBS They Make NO Demands
Paris May '68
AND THEN THEY BREAK UP ONE DAY AND GO BACK TO WORK, WITHOUT SO MUCH AS NODDING AGAIN AT THEIR NEIGHBORS.
THAT WAS PARIS IN '68. I WAS IN PARIS IN '85 WHEN MADONNA WAS JUST CATCHING ON—
BECAUSE ABOUT SOME THINGS THE FRENCH'RE SO BEHIND.
THE OLD WORLD IS BEHIND YOU
HISTORY
NO FUTURE
LIVE WITHOUT
85 madonna
BUT THEN ABOUT OTHER THINGS, THINGS LIKE THE LETTRISTS STARTING IN '52, THEY'RE THE FIRST, THE FRENCH ARE.

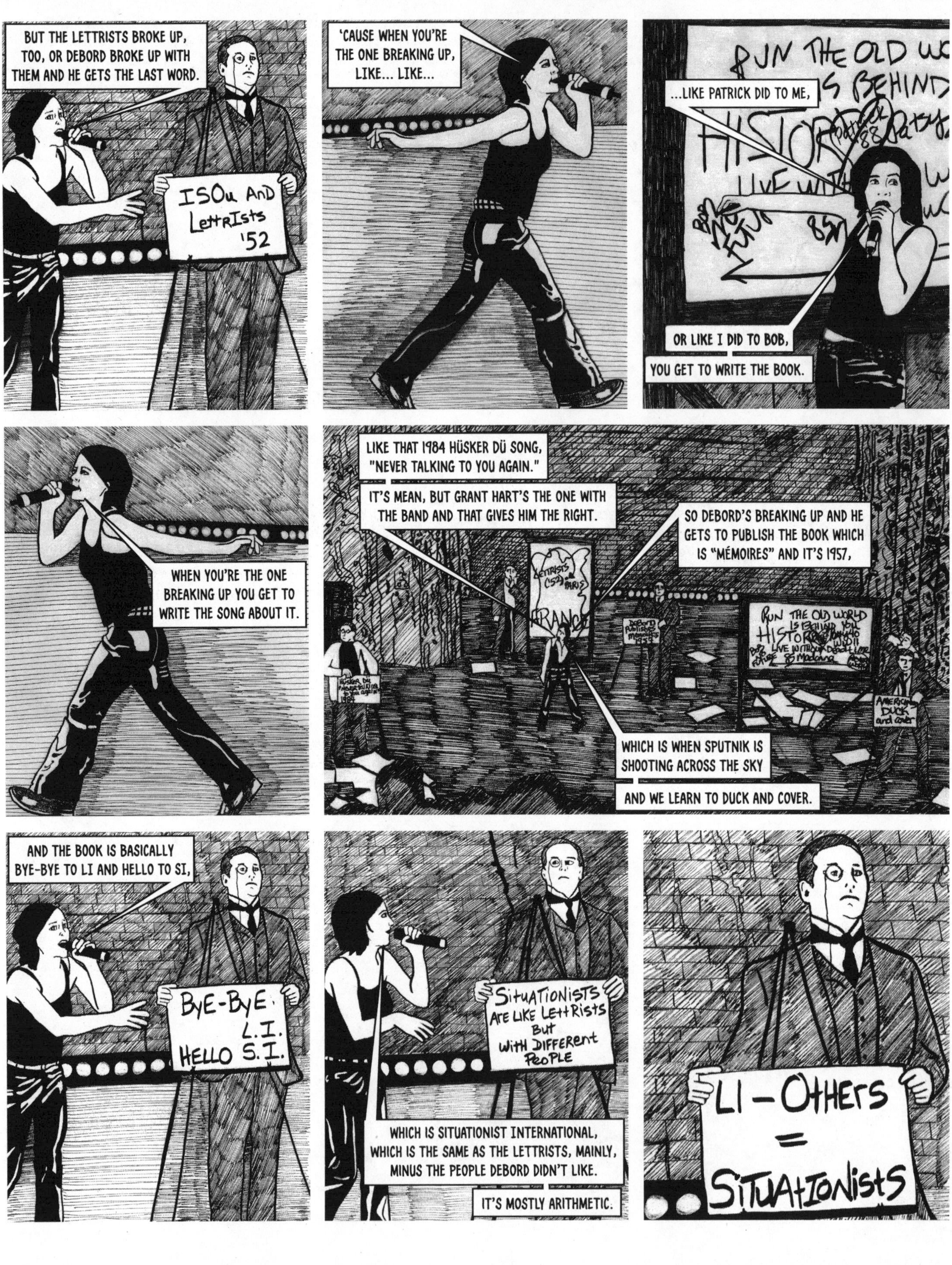
BUT THE LETTRISTS BROKE UP, TOO, OR DEBORD BROKE UP WITH THEM AND HE GETS THE LAST WORD.
ISOu AND LettRIsts '52
'CAUSE WHEN YOU'RE THE ONE BREAKING UP, LIKE... LIKE...
RUN THE OLD WO
S BEHIND
HISTOR
LIVE WITH
...LIKE PATRICK DID TO ME,
OR LIKE I DID TO BOB,
YOU GET TO WRITE THE BOOK.
WHEN YOU'RE THE ONE BREAKING UP YOU GET TO WRITE THE SONG ABOUT IT.
LIKE THAT 1984 HÜSKER DÜ SONG, "NEVER TALKING TO YOU AGAIN."
IT'S MEAN, BUT GRANT HART'S THE ONE WITH THE BAND AND THAT GIVES HIM THE RIGHT.
SO DEBORD'S BREAKING UP AND HE GETS TO PUBLISH THE BOOK WHICH IS "MÉMOIRES" AND IT'S 1957,
LETTRISTS ('52) PARIS
FRANCE
RUN THE OLD WORLD IS BEHIND
HISTORY
AMERICANS DUCK and cover
WHICH IS WHEN SPUTNIK IS SHOOTING ACROSS THE SKY
AND WE LEARN TO DUCK AND COVER.
AND THE BOOK IS BASICALLY BYE-BYE TO LI AND HELLO TO SI,
ByE-ByE L.I. HELLO S.I.
SituATIONists ARE LIKE LettRists But with DIFFERENT PeoPLE
WHICH IS SITUATIONIST INTERNATIONAL, WHICH IS THE SAME AS THE LETTRISTS, MAINLY, MINUS THE PEOPLE DEBORD DIDN'T LIKE.
IT'S MOSTLY ARITHMETIC.
LI – Others = SItUAtIONists

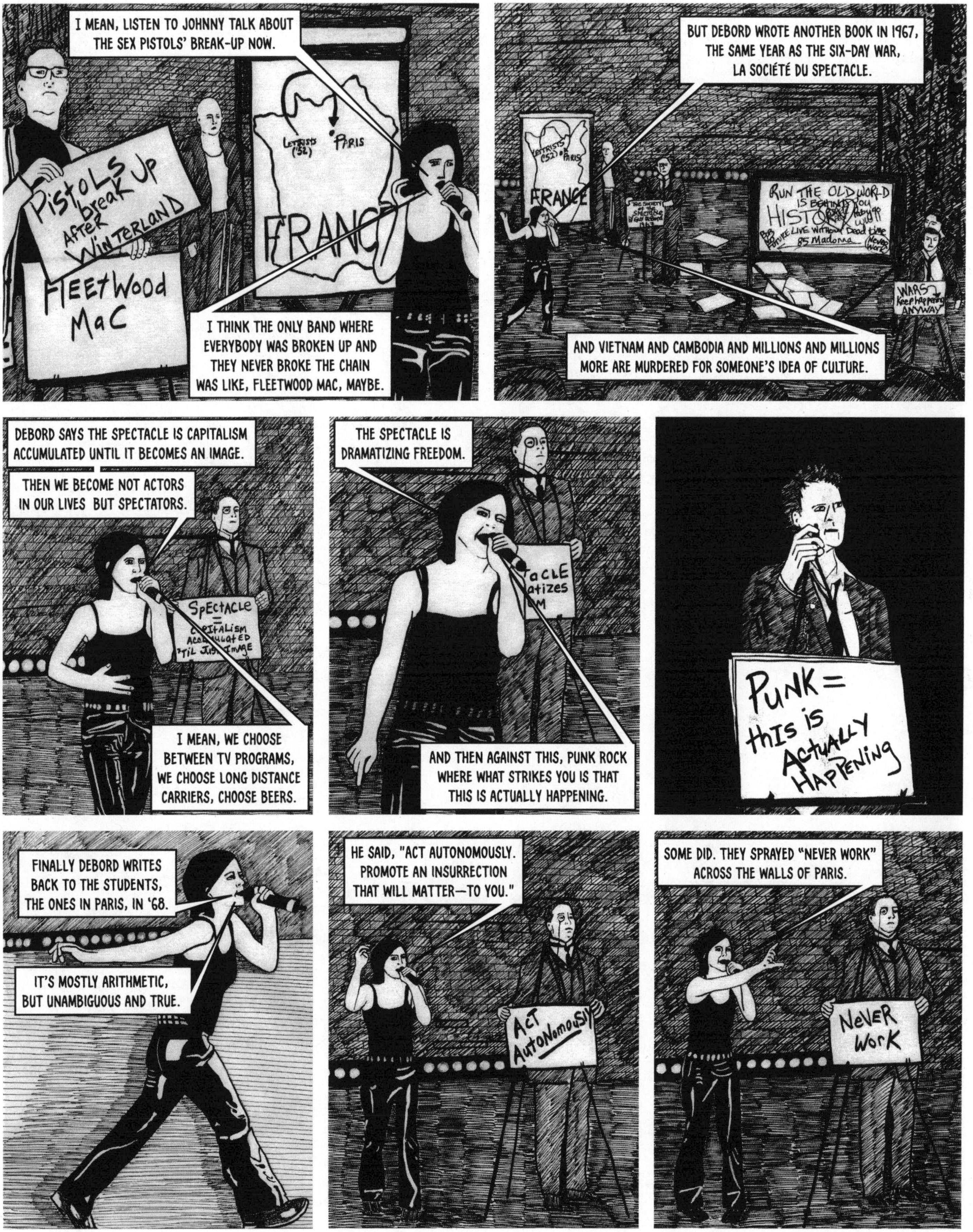
I MEAN, LISTEN TO JOHNNY TALK ABOUT THE SEX PISTOLS' BREAK-UP NOW.
PISTOLS break UP AFTER WINTERLAND
FLEETWOOD MAC
LETRISTS ('52)
PARIS
I THINK THE ONLY BAND WHERE EVERYBODY WAS BROKEN UP AND THEY NEVER BROKE THE CHAIN WAS LIKE, FLEETWOOD MAC, MAYBE.
BUT DEBORD WROTE ANOTHER BOOK IN 1967, THE SAME YEAR AS THE SIX-DAY WAR, LA SOCIÉTÉ DU SPECTACLE.
FRANCE
WARS Keep happening ANYWAY
AND VIETNAM AND CAMBODIA AND MILLIONS AND MILLIONS MORE ARE MURDERED FOR SOMEONE'S IDEA OF CULTURE.
DEBORD SAYS THE SPECTACLE IS CAPITALISM ACCUMULATED UNTIL IT BECOMES AN IMAGE.
THEN WE BECOME NOT ACTORS IN OUR LIVES BUT SPECTATORS.
SPECTACLE =
I MEAN, WE CHOOSE BETWEEN TV PROGRAMS, WE CHOOSE LONG DISTANCE CARRIERS, CHOOSE BEERS.
THE SPECTACLE IS DRAMATIZING FREEDOM.
AND THEN AGAINST THIS, PUNK ROCK WHERE WHAT STRIKES YOU IS THAT THIS IS ACTUALLY HAPPENING.
PUNK = this is Actually Happening
FINALLY DEBORD WRITES BACK TO THE STUDENTS, THE ONES IN PARIS, IN '68.
IT'S MOSTLY ARITHMETIC, BUT UNAMBIGUOUS AND TRUE.
HE SAID, "ACT AUTONOMOUSLY. PROMOTE AN INSURRECTION THAT WILL MATTER—TO YOU."
ACT AUTONOMOUSLY
SOME DID. THEY SPRAYED "NEVER WORK" ACROSS THE WALLS OF PARIS.
NEVER WORK

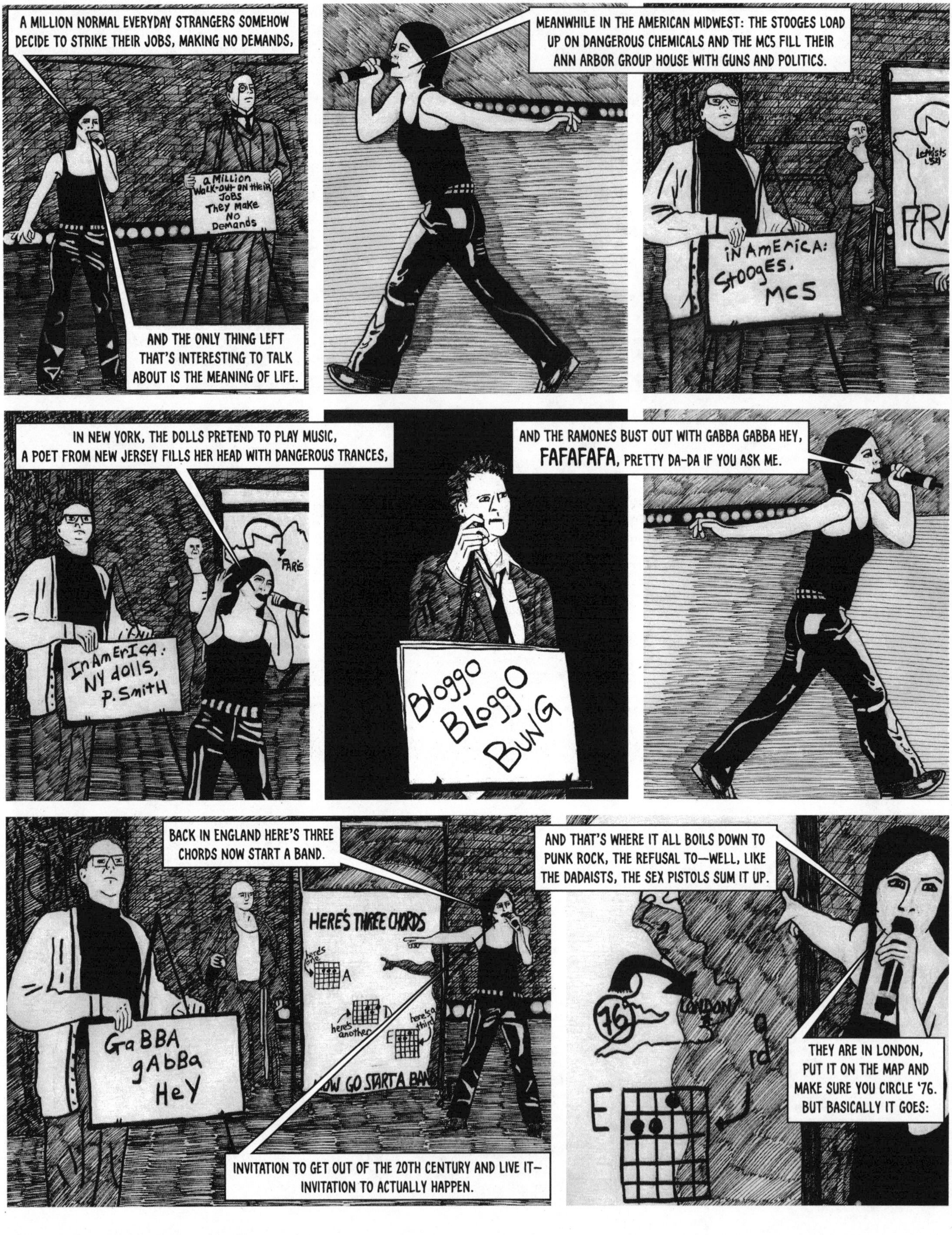

A MILLION NORMAL EVERYDAY STRANGERS SOMEHOW DECIDE TO STRIKE THEIR JOBS, MAKING NO DEMANDS,
a Million Walk-out on their Jobs They make No Demands
AND THE ONLY THING LEFT THAT'S INTERESTING TO TALK ABOUT IS THE MEANING OF LIFE.
MEANWHILE IN THE AMERICAN MIDWEST: THE STOOGES LOAD UP ON DANGEROUS CHEMICALS AND THE MC5 FILL THEIR ANN ARBOR GROUP HOUSE WITH GUNS AND POLITICS.
in America: Stooges. MC5
IN NEW YORK, THE DOLLS PRETEND TO PLAY MUSIC, A POET FROM NEW JERSEY FILLS HER HEAD WITH DANGEROUS TRANCES,
PARIS
In AmErica: NY dolls, P. Smith
Bloggo Bloggo Bung
AND THE RAMONES BUST OUT WITH GABBA GABBA HEY, **FAFAFAFA**, PRETTY DA-DA IF YOU ASK ME.
BACK IN ENGLAND HERE'S THREE CHORDS NOW START A BAND.
HERE'S THREE CHORDS
here's one
A
D
here's another
E
here's a third
GaBBA gAbBa HeY
INVITATION TO GET OUT OF THE 20TH CENTURY AND LIVE IT—INVITATION TO ACTUALLY HAPPEN.
AND THAT'S WHERE IT ALL BOILS DOWN TO PUNK ROCK, THE REFUSAL TO—WELL, LIKE THE DADAISTS, THE SEX PISTOLS SUM IT UP.
76
LONDON
E
THEY ARE IN LONDON, PUT IT ON THE MAP AND MAKE SURE YOU CIRCLE '76. BUT BASICALLY IT GOES:

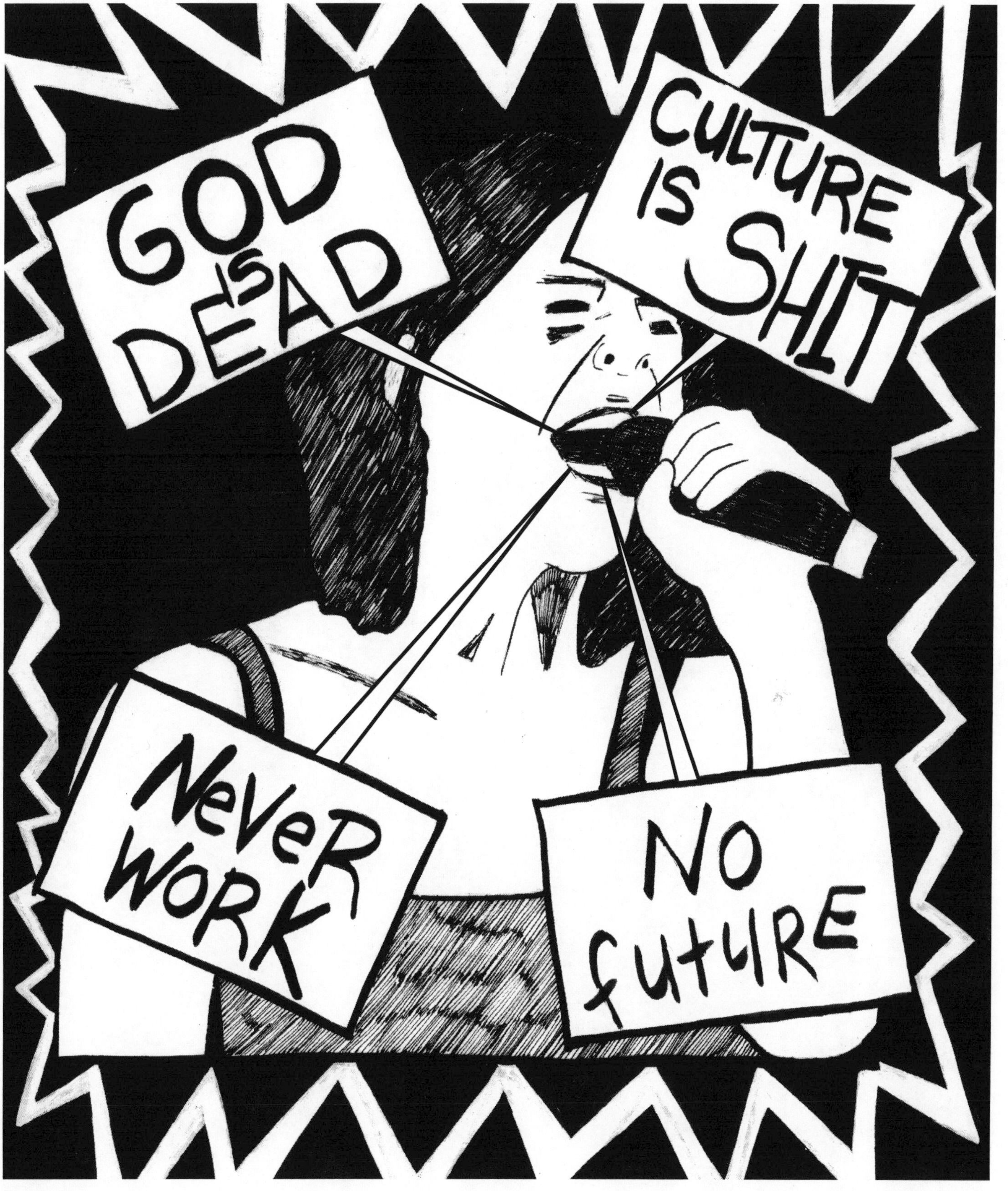
GOD IS DEAD
CULTURE IS SHIT
NeVeR WORK
NO future

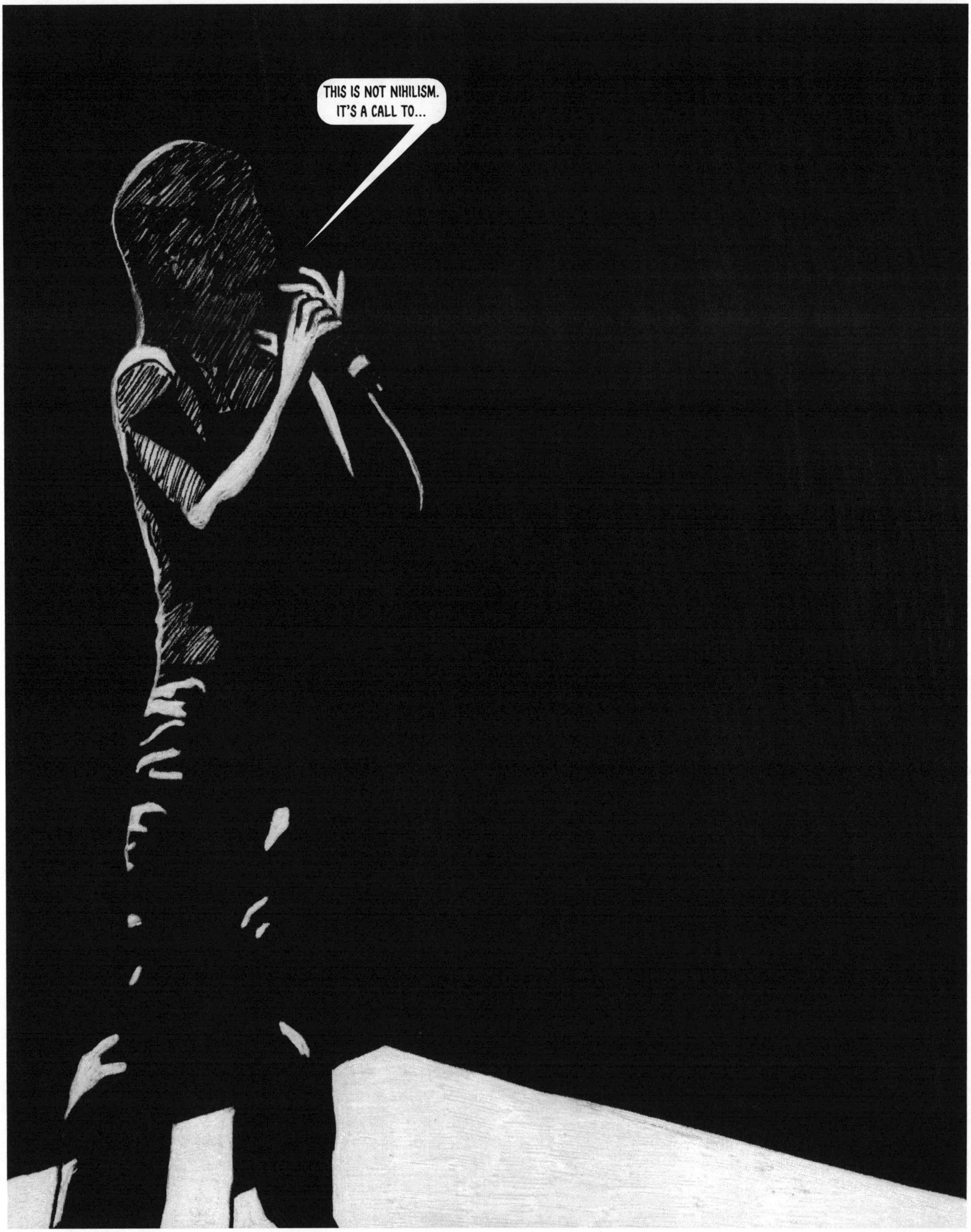
THIS IS NOT NIHILISM.
IT'S A CALL TO...

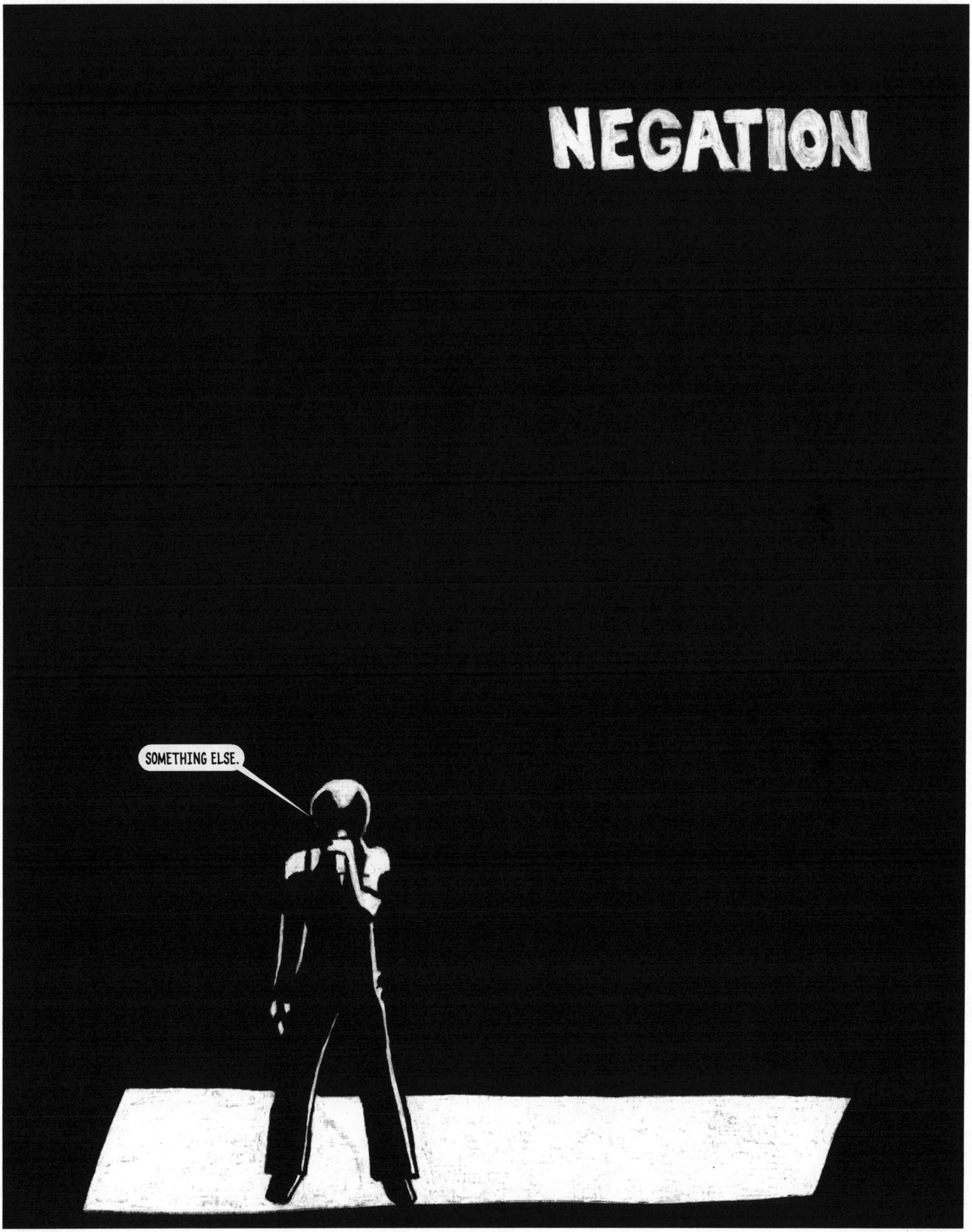
NEGATION
SOMETHING ELSE.

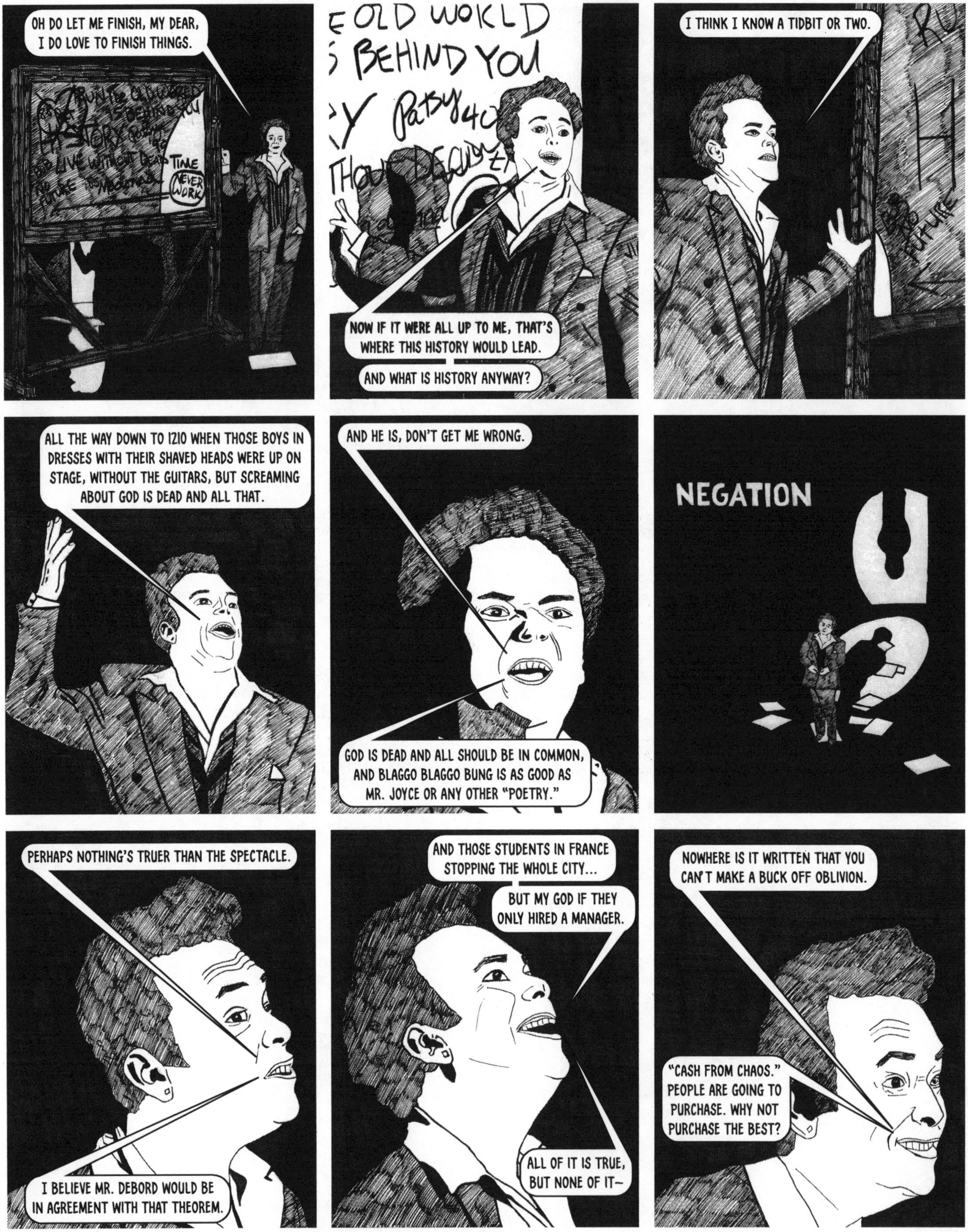
OH DO LET ME FINISH, MY DEAR, I DO LOVE TO FINISH THINGS.
NOW IF IT WERE ALL UP TO ME, THAT'S WHERE THIS HISTORY WOULD LEAD.
AND WHAT IS HISTORY ANYWAY?
I THINK I KNOW A TIDBIT OR TWO.
ALL THE WAY DOWN TO 1210 WHEN THOSE BOYS IN DRESSES WITH THEIR SHAVED HEADS WERE UP ON STAGE, WITHOUT THE GUITARS, BUT SCREAMING ABOUT GOD IS DEAD AND ALL THAT.
AND HE IS, DON'T GET ME WRONG.
GOD IS DEAD AND ALL SHOULD BE IN COMMON, AND BLAGGO BLAGGO BUNG IS AS GOOD AS MR. JOYCE OR ANY OTHER "POETRY."
NEGATION
PERHAPS NOTHING'S TRUER THAN THE SPECTACLE.
I BELIEVE MR. DEBORD WOULD BE IN AGREEMENT WITH THAT THEOREM.
AND THOSE STUDENTS IN FRANCE STOPPING THE WHOLE CITY...
BUT MY GOD IF THEY ONLY HIRED A MANAGER.
ALL OF IT IS TRUE, BUT NONE OF IT–
NOWHERE IS IT WRITTEN THAT YOU CAN'T MAKE A BUCK OFF OBLIVION.
"CASH FROM CHAOS." PEOPLE ARE GOING TO PURCHASE. WHY NOT PURCHASE THE BEST?

JOHNNY VOICED A NEAR ABSOLUTE LOATHING OF HIS TIME AND PLACE, AND THE NOTE HELD UNTIL DISGUST TURNED TO GLEE.

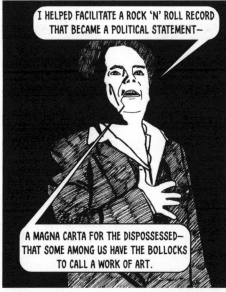

I HELPED FACILITATE A ROCK 'N' ROLL RECORD THAT BECAME A POLITICAL STATEMENT—

A MAGNA CARTA FOR THE DISPOSSESSED— THAT SOME AMONG US HAVE THE BOLLOCKS TO CALL A WORK OF ART.

ONE MIGHT PUT IT IN A MUSEUM, MIGHTN'T ONE?

IN CLEVELAND, OHIO, PERHAPS.

I'M A SHOPKEEPER THAT SOLD THE WORLD ITS OWN PICTURE, COMPLETE WITH GRUNT AND SCREAM.

THEY THINK IT'S ART, POLITICS, RELIGION, PUNK ROCK.

I THINK—WHY EVER THEY BUY IT—

IT'S 12 CENTS EVERY TIME.

WHAT'S HISTORY?

PERHAPS IT'S GETTING THE LAST WORD.

THANK YOU, MALCOLM.

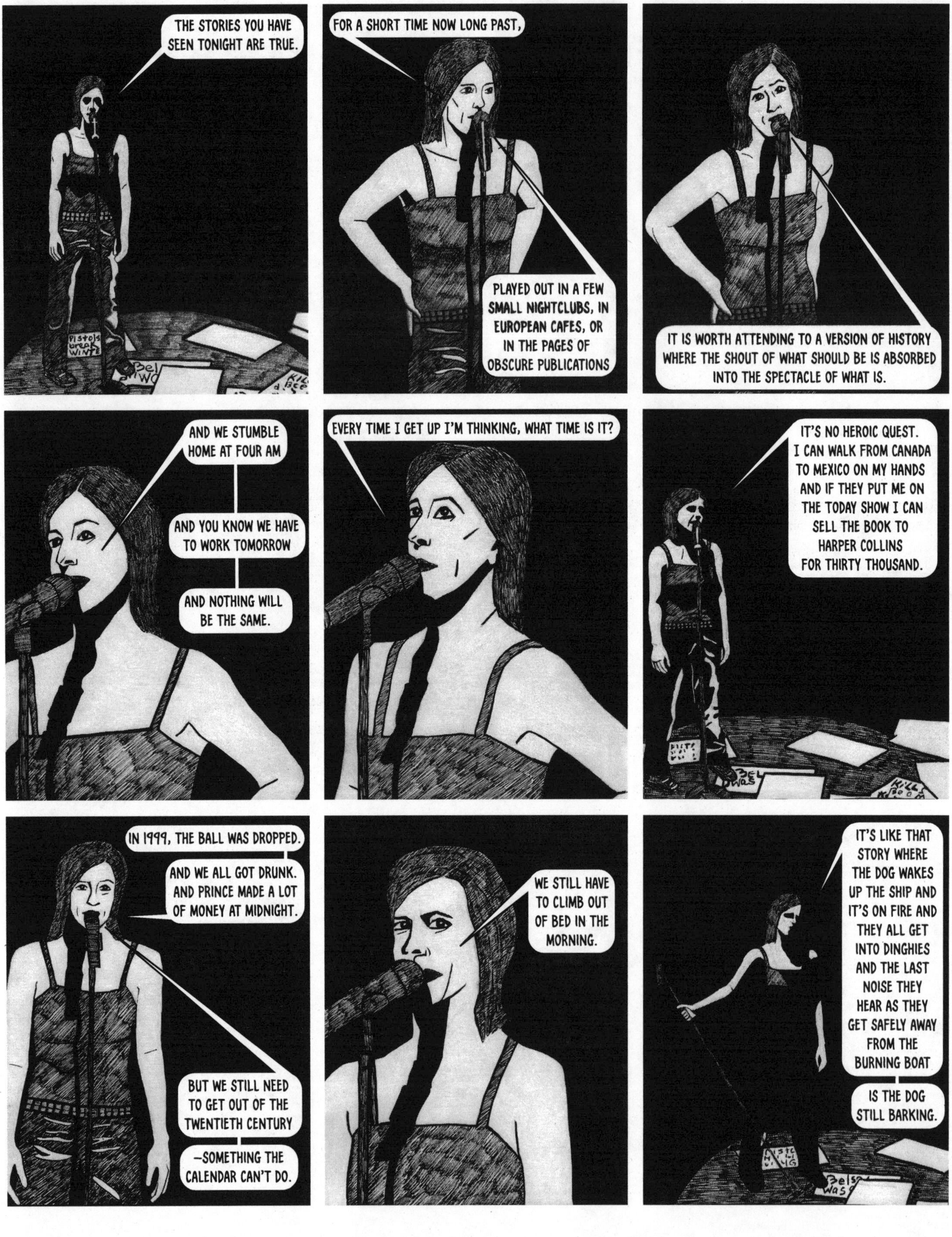
THE STORIES YOU HAVE SEEN TONIGHT ARE TRUE.
FOR A SHORT TIME NOW LONG PAST,
PLAYED OUT IN A FEW SMALL NIGHTCLUBS, IN EUROPEAN CAFES, OR IN THE PAGES OF OBSCURE PUBLICATIONS
IT IS WORTH ATTENDING TO A VERSION OF HISTORY WHERE THE SHOUT OF WHAT SHOULD BE IS ABSORBED INTO THE SPECTACLE OF WHAT IS.
AND WE STUMBLE HOME AT FOUR AM
AND YOU KNOW WE HAVE TO WORK TOMORROW
AND NOTHING WILL BE THE SAME.
EVERY TIME I GET UP I'M THINKING, WHAT TIME IS IT?
IT'S NO HEROIC QUEST. I CAN WALK FROM CANADA TO MEXICO ON MY HANDS AND IF THEY PUT ME ON THE TODAY SHOW I CAN SELL THE BOOK TO HARPER COLLINS FOR THIRTY THOUSAND.
IN 1999, THE BALL WAS DROPPED.
AND WE ALL GOT DRUNK. AND PRINCE MADE A LOT OF MONEY AT MIDNIGHT.
BUT WE STILL NEED TO GET OUT OF THE TWENTIETH CENTURY
—SOMETHING THE CALENDAR CAN'T DO.
WE STILL HAVE TO CLIMB OUT OF BED IN THE MORNING.
IT'S LIKE THAT STORY WHERE THE DOG WAKES UP THE SHIP AND IT'S ON FIRE AND THEY ALL GET INTO DINGHIES AND THE LAST NOISE THEY HEAR AS THEY GET SAFELY AWAY FROM THE BURNING BOAT
IS THE DOG STILL BARKING.

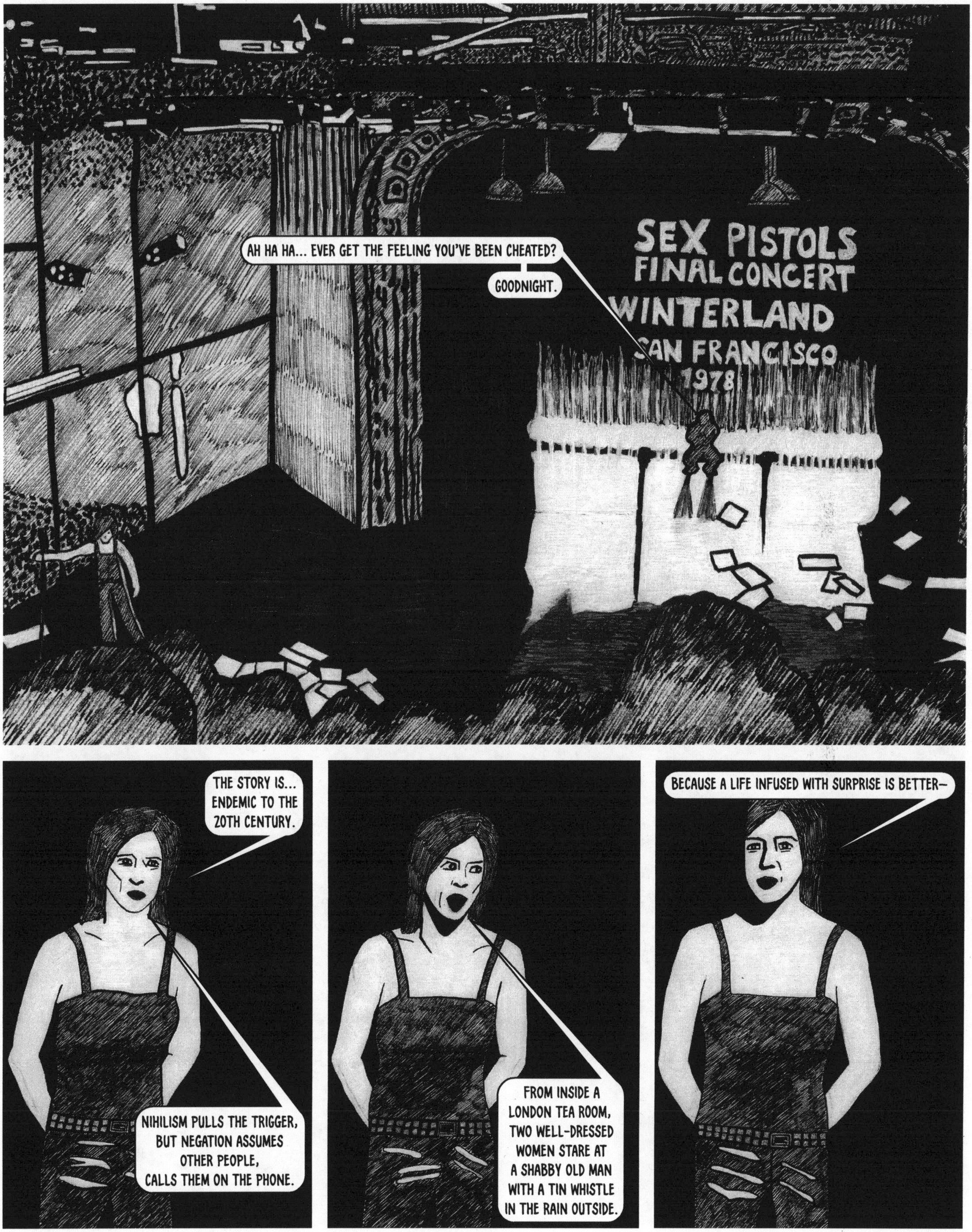
AH HA HA... EVER GET THE FEELING YOU'VE BEEN CHEATED?
GOODNIGHT.
SEX PISTOLS FINAL CONCERT WINTERLAND SAN FRANCISCO 1978
THE STORY IS... ENDEMIC TO THE 20TH CENTURY.
NIHILISM PULLS THE TRIGGER, BUT NEGATION ASSUMES OTHER PEOPLE, CALLS THEM ON THE PHONE.
FROM INSIDE A LONDON TEA ROOM, TWO WELL-DRESSED WOMEN STARE AT A SHABBY OLD MAN WITH A TIN WHISTLE IN THE RAIN OUTSIDE.
BECAUSE A LIFE INFUSED WITH SURPRISE IS BETTER—

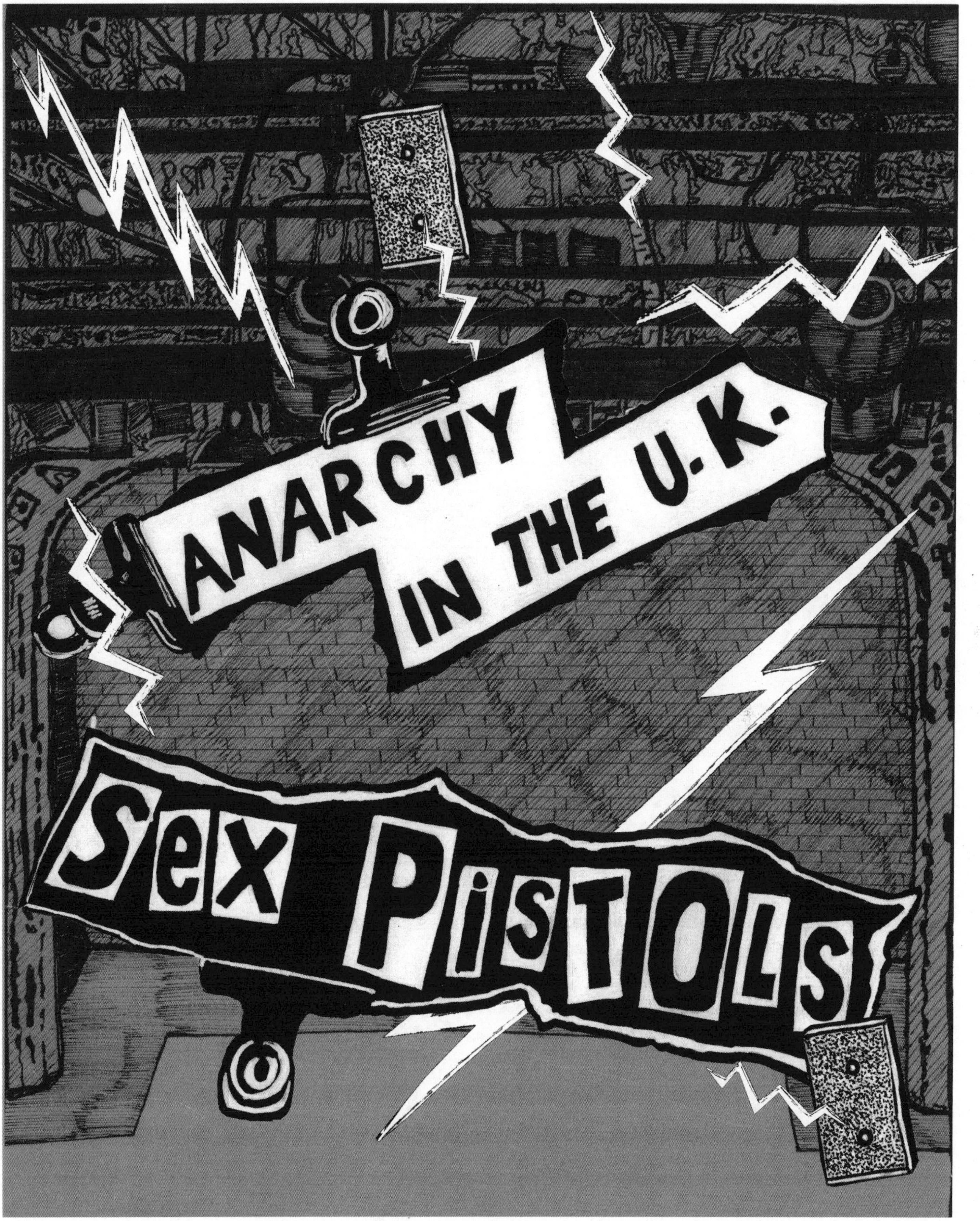
ANARCHY
IN THE U.K.
SEX PISTOLS

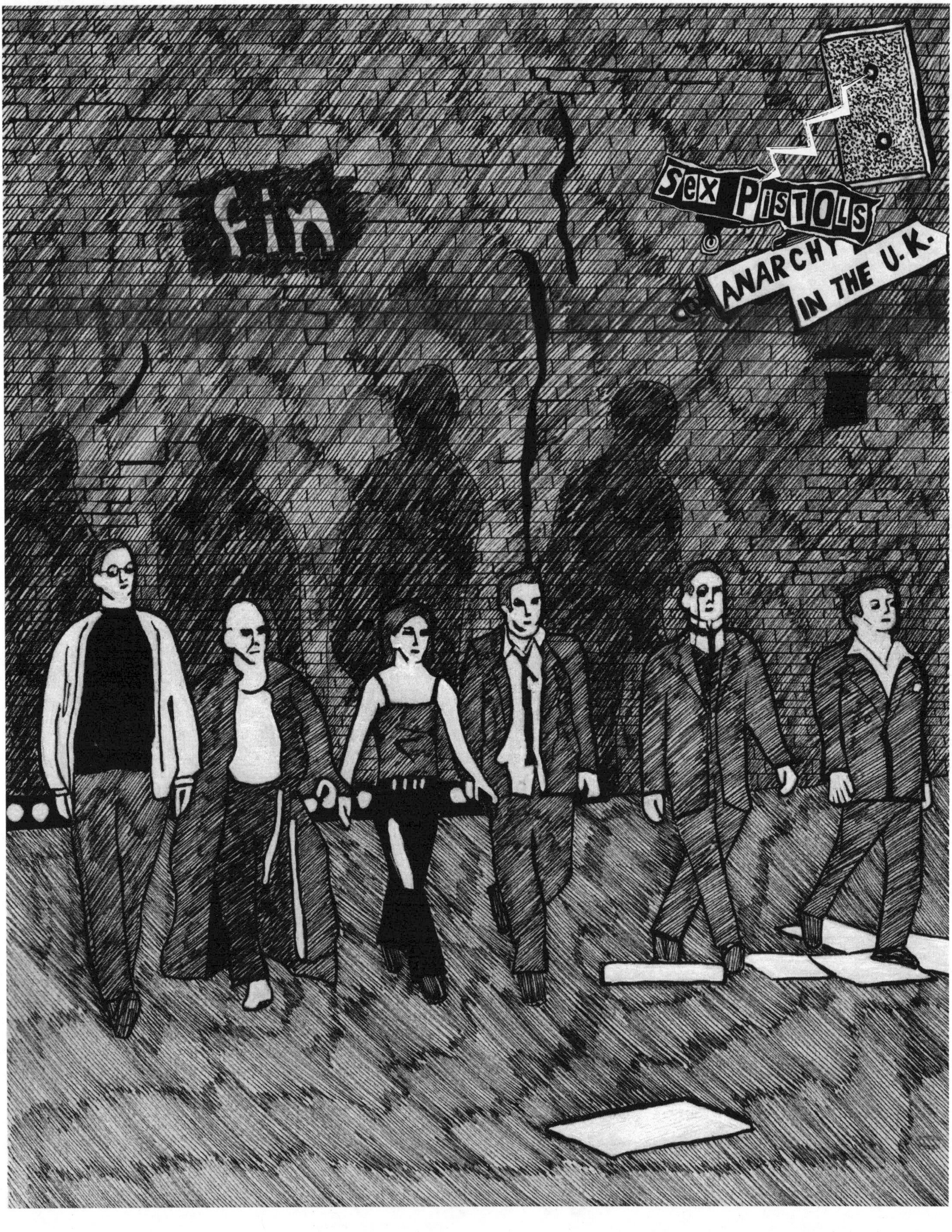
fin
SEX PISTOLS
ANARCHY IN THE U.K.

ABOUT RUDE MECHS

Rude Mechs is an Austin, Texas-based theatre collective that has created a genre-averse slate of roughly 30 new plays since 1996. What these works hold in common are the use of play to make performance, the use of theatres as meeting places for audience and artists, and the use of humor as a tool for intellectual investigation. Rude Mechs' touring productions include **The Method Gun**, **Not Every Mountain** (finishing commission from The Guthrie Theatre), **Stop Hitting Yourself** (commissioned by Lincoln Center Theatre's LCT3), **Field Guide** (commissioned by Yale Repertory Theatre's Binger Center for New Works), **I've Never Been So Happy** (finishing commission from Center Theatre Group), **Get Your War On**, **Now Now Oh Now**, **How Late It Was, How Late**, **Match-Play**, **Cherrywood**, and **Lipstick Traces**.

Co-Producing Artistic Directors: Madge Darlington, Thomas Graves, Lana Lesley, Kirk Lynn, and Shawn Sides.

LIPSTICK TRACES: A SECRET HISTORY OF THE TWENTIETH CENTURY

Created by Rude Mechs

Conceived and Directed by Shawn Sides

Adapted by Kirk Lynn from the eponymous book by Greil Marcus

Lipstick Traces was originally work-shopped in August 1999 at The Ohio Theatre's Ice Factory Festival in New York, then premiered at The Off Center in Austin, TX in September 1999, and was remounted there in September 2000. Foundry Theatre produced the off-Broadway premiere in May 2001 at The Ohio Theatre.

Lipstick Traces toured to The Walker Art Center (Minneapolis, MN), DiverseWorks (Houston, TX), The Wexner Center for the Arts (Columbus, OH), CSPS/Legion Arts (Cedar Rapids, IA), On The Boards (Seattle, WA), UCLA Live! (Los Angeles, CA) and Szene Salzburg Festival (Salzburg, Austria).

ORIGINAL CAST
Dr. Narrator / Souxsie Sioux – Lana Lesley
Malcolm McLaren / Bill Grundy – Ehren Conner Christian
Johnny Rotten – E. Jason Liebrecht
John of Leyden / Michel Mourre / Tristan Tzara / Paul Cook – Michael T. Mergen
Guy Debord / Hugo Ball / Steve Jones – Gavin Mundy
Richard Huelsenbeck / Glen Matlock – Robert Pierson

ORIGINAL PRODUCTION TEAM
Assistant Director – Brad Beckman
Lighting Design – Zach Murphy
Costume Design – Marit Aagaard
Scenic Design – Ann Marie Gordon, Gavin Mundy
Sound Design – Gordon Gunn and Darron L West
Production Stage Manager – Dave Reed

RUDE MECHS TOURING TEAM
Walker, Wexner, CSPS, DiverseWorks, Szene Salzburg
Dr. Narrator / Sioux - Lana Lesley
McLaren / Grundy - Ehren Christian
McLaren / Grundy - Henry Stram (Salzburg)
Rotten - E. Jason Liebrecht
Leyden / Cook / Tzara- Michael T. Mergen
Debord / Ball / Jones - Jason Phelps
Debord / Ball / Jones- James Urbaniak (Salzburg)
Huelsenbeck / Matlock - Robert Pierson
Lighting Design - Brian H Scott
Scenic Design - Anne Marie Gordon
Scenic Design / Technical Director - Madge Darlington
Associate Lighting Designer - Zak Al-Alami
Sound Engineer - Sunil Rajan
Stage Manager - Jenny Slattery
Assistant Stage Manager - José Angel Hernández
Tour Manager - Sarah Richardson

FOUNDRY CAST
Dr. Narrator / Sioux - Lana Lesley
McLaren / Grundy - David Greenspan
Rotten - E. Jason Liebrecht
Leyden / Mourre / Tzara - Ean Sheehy
Debord / Ball / Jones - James Urbaniak
Huelsenbeck - T. Ryder Smith

FOUNDRY PRODUCTION TEAM
Producer / Artistic Director - Melanie Joseph
Lighting Design - Heather Carson
Sound Design - Darron L West
Set Design - Jim Larkin, Madge Darlington
Costume Design - Rachel Carr
Stage Manager - Sarah Richardson

FOUNDRY TOURING TEAM
UCLA Live! and On The Boards
Dr. Narrator / Sioux - Lana Lesley
McLaren / Grundy – Henry Stram
Rotten - E. Jason Liebrecht
Leyden / Mourre / Tzara – Darren Pettie
Debord / Ball / Jones – Randolph Curtis Rand
Huelsenbeck / Matlock - T. Ryder Smith
Lighting Design - Brian H Scott
Production Stage Manager - Sarah Richardson

LIPSTICK TRACES:
A SECRET HISTORY OF THE TWENTIETH CENTURY

FEATURING

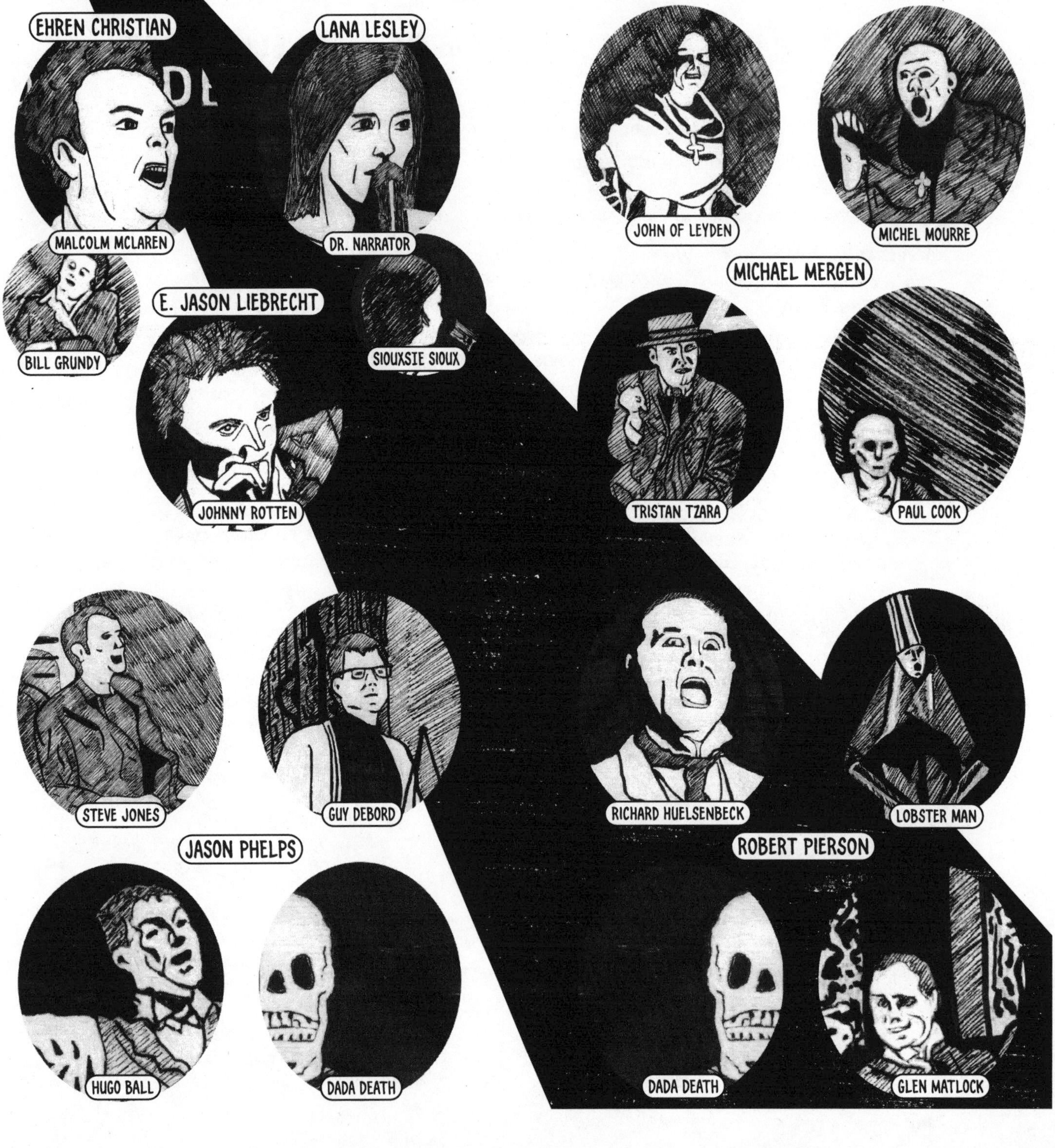
EHREN CHRISTIAN
MALCOLM MCLAREN
BILL GRUNDY
LANA LESLEY
DR. NARRATOR
E. JASON LIEBRECHT
JOHNNY ROTTEN
SIOUXSIE SIOUX
JOHN OF LEYDEN
MICHEL MOURRE
MICHAEL MERGEN
TRISTAN TZARA
PAUL COOK
STEVE JONES
GUY DEBORD
RICHARD HUELSENBECK
LOBSTER MAN
JASON PHELPS
HUGO BALL
DADA DEATH
ROBERT PIERSON
DADA DEATH
GLEN MATLOCK

ACKNOWLEDGMENTS

RUDE MECHS THANKS

The entire project begins and ends with the generosity, love, spirt and support of Greil Marcus.
It has been a privilege to get to know him and his lovely family,
and we feel wildly lucky to call him a friend.
Thank you, Greil.

And thank you to Emily Forland and Rick Pappas for clearing paths and being on team Rude!

Special love and thanks to Philip Bither of the Walker Arts Center for helping Rude Mechs book our
first-ever national tour, and for presenting **Lipstick Traces** in January 2002
at The Southern Theater, where this book is set.

Love and gratitude to Melanie Joseph for her faith and support, for doing the often thankless and
always difficult job of producing the play, for giving us our first-ever off-Broadway production, and
our first-ever west coast tour, and for putting her whole heart into every single second of it.

Special thanks to everyone that helped us write the play, make the play, make the play better,
produce the play, and tour the play: Robert Arjet, Brad Beckman, David Bucci, CSPS / Legion Arts,
Lane Czaplinski / On The Boards, Anne Engelking, Tim Fisk, Emily Forland, Josh Frank,
Catherine Glynn, David Greenspan, Chuck Helm / The Wexner, Kimberlee Hewitt, Morgan Knicely,
Jim Larkin, Robert Lyons / The Ohio Theatre, Malcolm McLaren, Darren Pettie, Stephen Pruitt,
Mark Russell, Peggy Shaw, Ean Sheehy, T. Ryder Smith, Henry Stram, James Urbaniak,
Sixto Wagan / DiverseWorks, Wendy Weil, and David Sefton / UCLA Live!,
and to Katey Gilligan, we miss you.

LANA THANKS

This book would not have been possible without the generous support of the following people who
carved out time and space for me to work in their precious spaces: Patsy Lesley,
Bonnie Reese & Erik Rune, Tina Harrison-Linklater & Rick Linklater, and
Liz Engelman at the Tofte Lake Center.

To Rick Pappas, I have no words for how amazing and supportive and cool you are.
I just feel so lucky to count you as a friend.

Forever love to Shawn, Kirk, Madge, Thomas and Alex for the crazy freedom to do
just whatever the fuck I wanted with this project.

And crazy solid yays and thank yous to 53rd State Press for waiting so patiently and supportively
while I worked in tiny fits and jagged spurts between projects, tours, giving up, and real life.

And to Peter Stopschinski, thank you for listening to me, supporting me and giving me courage,
advice, and amazing feedback. You are the most creative and generous person I know.

ALSO FROM 53rd STATE PRESS

The Book of the Dog // Karinne Keithley
Joyce Cho Plays // Joyce Cho
No Dice // Nature Theater of Oklahoma
When You Rise Up // Miguel Gutierrez
Montgomery Park, or Opulence // Karinne Keithley
Crime or Emergency // Sibyl Kempson
Off the Hozzle // Rob Erickson
A Map of Virtue + Black Cat Lost // Erin Courtney
Pig Iron: Three Plays // Pig Iron Theatre Company
The Mayor of Baltimore + Anthem // Kristen Kosmas
Ich, Kürbisgeist + The Secret Death of Puppets // Sibyl Kempson
Soulographie: Our Genocides // Erik Ehn
Life and Times: Episode 1 // Nature Theater of Oklahoma
Life and Times: Episode 2 // Nature Theater of Oklahoma
Life and Times: Episode 3 + 4 // Nature Theater of Oklahoma
The 53rd State Occasional No. 1 // Ed. Paul Lazar
There There // Kristen Kosmas
Seagull (Thinking of You) // Tina Satter
Self Made Man Man Made Land // Ursula Eagly
Another Telepathic Thing // Big Dance Theater
Another Tree Dance // Karinne Keithley Syers
Let Us Now Praise Susan Sontag // Sibyl Kempson
Dance by Letter // Annie-B Parson
Pop Star Series // Neal Medlyn
The Javier Plays // Carlos Murillo
Minor Theater: Three Plays // Julia Jarcho
Ghost Rings (12-inch vinyl) // Half Straddle
A New Practical Guide to Rhetorical Gesture and Action // NTUSA
A Field Guide to iLANDing // iLAND
The 53rd State Occasional No. 2 // Ed. Will Arbery
Suicide Forest // Kristine Haruna Lee
Lipstick Traces // Lana Lesley + Rude Mechs

FORTHCOMING

Best Behavior // David Levine
A Discourse on Method // David Levine + Shonni Enelow
I Understand Everything Better // David Neumann + Sibyl Kempson
Milton // PearlDamour
Wood Calls Out to Wood // Corinne Donly
ASTRS // Karinne Keithley
The People's Republic of Valerie // Kristen Kosmas
WATER SPORTS; or insignificant white boys // Jeremy O. Harris